THE ANGLER'S COAST

THE ANGLER'S COAST

RUSSELL CHATHAM

with illustrations by the author

Introduction by Thomas McGuane

DOUBLEDAY & COMPANY, INC., GARDEN CITY, NEW YORK   1976

Some of these stories were previously published in the following publications: *The Atlantic Monthly,* WADING FOR GODOT, Copyright © 1976 by The Atlantic Monthly Company; *Sports Illustrated,* NO WIND IN THE WILLOWS as BY THE CELLBLOCKS AND THE BAY and HERRING IS BELIEVING as HORS D'OEUVRES FOR THE ANXIOUS ANGLER, Copyright © 1973 by Time, Inc., and DESERT TROUT as GAMBLING YOUR LIFE AWAY and BEHOLD THE FISHERMAN as THE WORLD'S BEST, Copyright © 1974 by Time, Inc.; *True Magazine,* NIGHT OF THE SALMON, Copyright © 1973 by Fawcett Publications, Inc.; *Outdoor Life,* TO CATCH A STEELHEAD as STEELHEAD ON THE FLY, Copyright © 1974 by Times Mirror Magazines, Inc.; *Sports Afield,* A CERTAIN MOMENT as FISHERMAN'S TWILIGHT, Copyright © 1976 by The Hearst Corp.; *Sports Afield Fishing Annual,* 1976 Edition, TIME AND TIDE as APPOINTMENT WITH THE TIDE, Copyright © 1976 by The Hearst Corp.

The story HARD AS A ROCK first appeared in *California Living Magazine.*

Library of Congress Cataloging in Publication Data

Chatham, Russell.
The angler's coast.

CONTENTS: Behold the fisherman.—A certain moment.—Hard as a rock. [etc.]
1. Fly-fishing.   2. Fishing—Northwest, Pacific.
3. Fishing—California.   I. Title.
SH456.C48   799.1′2
ISBN 0-385-00946-1
Library of Congress Catalog Card Number 74–18786

For Phil Wood

*—And this is no small thing, for
in all its history angling has
brought delight and pleasure to
many and harm to no one.*

Roderick L. Haig-Brown

CONTENTS

FORK IT OVER:
a prologue to Russell Chatham

Russell Chatham's unfocused sense of alarm and abrupt changes of direction leave, in one volume, fish, fisherman and reader in a state of deep confusion. What is it that he wants?

Some angling writers have traveled the world over in search of big fish; Chatham has *cruised*. And you, dear reader, may be the last to buy it.

Chatham has seen it all; he's seen the bottom-bumpers flog-
ging fresh-run steelhead with spoons as big as the Ritz. He
has found sweet redemption, fishing myopically for herring in
the shadows of the Golden State's satanic villages where the
Symbionese Liberation Army has seized the split bamboo.
And in one stroke—an account of the taking of a world's
record striped bass at San Quentin—he gives us a more complete picture, a more beautiful one, certainly, of the hit-and-
run state of the art for today's angling fanatic.

The serene end of the spectrum is not absent from this
book; it's just that the valhallas are not where they're sup-
posed to be, at the end of expensive floatplane rides, splitting
the fare with an orthodontist and his credit cards, or a feed-
lot owner and two chorus girls. The magic zone keeps turning
out to be a rectangle of light made by a highway bridge lamp
where stripers crack into the holding bait; or a desolate im-
poundment in the Nevada desert where cutthroats go on
about their business. It sometimes turns out to be an adjust-
ment of the mind or a change of scale so that the six-inchers
charging the fly change your rate of pulse much as the bonzai
blue-water forays of Zane Grey did.

Chatham knows everything has gone to hell just as well as
you do. Somehow, this book shows you how it hasn't gotten
to him. The invitation it proffers is to extract yourself from
the brochure-exotic of the hunting-and-fishing magazines and
speculate on whatever game is actually in town. Take shots at
bigger things but keep your standards: scream with fear at
herring and bluegills; know the drama of small potatoes. The
"danger" of big-game fishing was never sufficient to unnerve
the starlets of La Paz, anyway. Bing Crosby comes back year
after year with his marlin rods, alive and well.

Taking any fish is an abstract puzzle, a game we'd sooner

play in amiable surroundings; but one we'll play in any case. No one would own up to matching wits with a shad or herring; but unraveling the skein of natural influence that is summarized in the little silver bugger's finally opening his mouth to your best effort, is, in effect, a kind of salute; beyond in all respects plunging a harpoon or treble hook into *anything*. It is an act of reverence and insinuation, with or without the floatplane and chorus girls.

As a book about fishing that lays the groundwork for going on at all with this superior enterprise in our epoch, Russell Chatham's has everything to recommend it.

THOMAS MCGUANE

THE ANGLER'S COAST

Chapter One

BEHOLD THE FISHERMAN

If you drive north from San Francisco on the Redwood Highway, you pass through the alluvial landscape of Marin and southern Sonoma counties quickly and come upon the broad Santa Rosa Plain with its scattered oaks, rows of eucalyptus and occasional evergreens. The road parallels the Russian River near Cloverdale, slicing through lush vineyards, and then the mountains rise sharply in ever-thickening stands of fir and redwood. Beyond Willits, you begin to drop into the implacable Eel River Canyon where northern California really begins.

One night some years ago I sped up this road at eighty miles an hour in a newly acquired Citroën sedan. The trees stood blackly against a lucent sky as I plummeted along the South Fork, highway reflectors blasting by in continuing scintillas, reflecting my eagerness to reach the Smith River and join Bill Schaadt for a week of salmon fishing.

I twisted unappreciatively through the Prairie Creek groves, careened irresponsibly around a log truck and pressed into the dark. When I finally shut the car off it exhaled and settled in the manner of its breed and the metal tinked and creaked with relief. Schaadt's trailer was dark so I stood for a moment listening to the sounds of the mill away to the north in the town of Smith River. By the light of a thin moon I read the lettering on the front of the trailer: TRAVELO-PASASALTA, CALIF.

Suddenly there was a squeal of tires and spray of gravel as a green Plymouth skidded into the narrow road and veered in beside the trailer. The door flew open and Bill was striding toward me, manic and thrashing.

"When you get in?"

"Minute ago."

"You hit it! Look."

He opened the car trunk to reveal three immense king salmon, the smallest of which would weigh well above thirty-five pounds.

Inside, the trailer was warm and familiar as Bill began making a pot of coffee. Fly lines hung from pegs and fly-tying tools lay on a crowded shelf along with many boxes of flies.

Half a dozen spare rods were tied to the ceiling.

Bill began to recount his day with infinite and dramatic detail. His tremendous, expressive hands flew through the cramped enclosure like bats in a lighted room as the gestures of casting, hooking and fighting many large fish made the events come alive.

Bill's eyes would focus on imagined water somewhere beyond the bed. Transported, he'd turn to follow the progress of his line downstream until a salmon took, then he'd outline the peculiarities of the struggle as he battled the lunging monster to a standstill near the sink.

In the morning we would fish the Early Hole. At the time it was the finest pool on the river with its impressive hundred-foot depths, mysterious grottos and inaccessibility.

It was late when we went to bed and as always Bill was asleep in minutes while I lay awake anticipating the dawn. Once again I was delightfully under the spell of the one man I know whose every thought, action and possession is a cohesive, unified extension of himself, like spokes in a wheel coming in perfect contact with the enclosing rim. Staring at little streaks of reflected light, my thoughts coursed back over the years to a time when I did not know Bill Schaadt.

My childhood was characterized by two obsessions: painting and fishing. The first was a rather private deviation, part of the family tradition. The second manifested itself in the form of a large account at the local sport shop.

My cousin and I spent part of each summer on the Russian River in his parents' cabin. It was during our first shad season in the early fifties that we started hearing of a fisherman named Bill Schaadt. The name is pronounced shad, like the fish, and not knowing at the time about the German spelling, we thought that man and fish were named alike. Besides, Schaadt is a sign painter and he signs his work SHAD SIGNS.

In the Russian River resort area, there are numerous billboards all along the roads. Everywhere we went there was a Shad Sign and the work was distinctive so if you looked at all, you could easily spot it from a distance. It was always a thrill to discover a new one. The high point came one year when Schaadt repainted all the store fronts in the town of Guerneville, thereby setting a kind of omnipresent Schaadt mood.

Everywhere we went along the river, after it was learned that we were fishing, the standard question would be asked. "Have you seen Bill Schaadt?" An article appeared by the venerable Ted Trueblood telling about the new sport of flyfishing for shad on the Russian River. The story was also about Schaadt the man. We read it with more than average interest and in our active imaginations it wasn't long before the legend was in full bloom.

We began to stalk Schaadt, who drove a distinctive 1937 black Dodge, which he had striped elaborately throughout. After a time he was forced to hide this car and also take other measures to avoid people like us who followed him constantly, hoping he'd lead them to fish.

Bill would even go to a poor spot and when he was sure a gallery of people were watching from a distance, pretend to hook and play a fish. Then, from inside his waders he'd surreptitiously withdraw a large cardboard cutout carried for the purpose of completing this ploy. He'd land the paper dummy, "release" it, slip it quickly back into his waders and go on fishing. As soon as people began to appear he'd reel in and sneak off to the place he really wanted to be all along.

But my cousin and I were not particularly interested in being led toward good fishing. In fact, it would have been an embarrassment. To us Schaadt was a hero. When we'd see his car parked along the river we would stop and peer through the trees searching for the solitary figure who practiced the art of fly-fishing so dynamically.

One spring much later I was with a friend shad fishing on the Russian River. My companion was older than I and had known Schaadt for years.

"I think you should meet Bill," he said. "Liking to fish the way you do. Let's go down to Monte Rio."

I looked forward to this event with much the same excitement others reserve for their wedding night. I was in awe as we pulled up in front of a small house set back against the hill beneath a massive oak tree. In front were any number of boats and old cars. The yard was full of lumber and signs, some finished, some in various states of completion and some discarded. From beneath a canvas awning where he had been working, a tall, dark, curly-headed man ambled forward to greet us. Initially his manner was guarded. Then he offered his immense hand.

By the time I awoke, Bill was moving around the trailer with a sense of urgency. He had already dressed, shaved and made coffee.

"Not much time," he said sternly as he whisked a frying pan onto the stove and deftly began fixing bacon and potatoes. While these cooked he made us each a lunch of leftover chicken, cheese, apples, cookies and a Thermos of coffee.

In moments the table was folded out, toast made, plates heated and eggs fried, then Bill set a perfect breakfast in front of me with a fresh cup of coffee.

I knew better than to offer assistance. In more than a decade and a half of fishing with Bill he has always cooked my breakfast and seen to it that I had a lunch, not because I couldn't do these things for myself, but because he is organized to do them more quickly. On rare occasions, I have been allowed to do the dishes.

Over coffee, Bill was like a general mapping out a campaign as he decided our moves. The road in to the Early was not well known.

"My boat's already there," he said. "We'll take your boat on my car around to the Walker Hole and row down. After today we'll walk in from the other side and no one will know how we got in. I've got another boat down at the Bailey Hole big enough for both of us if we decide to fish there later."

Bursting out of the trailer he rummaged in his car for rope while I untied my boat. We lifted it onto his racks and Bill lashed it down. I knew what to expect on these mornings so my tackle was rigged for fishing and I only had to remember a box of flies, leader, some spare lines and I was ready.

As we careened along the narrow North Bank Road at an intimidating speed, I thought about the time Bill had rolled his car over down on the Eel. He was almost where he was going so he crawled out, dragging his fly rod with him and hiked to the spot he had chosen on the river. That night, the fishing day over, he had a tow truck come and right his car.

It was also on the Eel that Schaadt had once found a deep pocket full of salmon which was surrounded by impenetrable snags. There was no way to get a cast in there. So one morning when no one was around, Bill rowed out with a long limb saw and cut a slot through the branches wide enough to let a fly line sink down to the fish. From then on he hooked all he could handle and even though most were lost to the snags he had constant action with no one else able to crowd in.

It was still dark when Bill found the obscure, rutted road to the river that angled through immense redwood groves. Within moments after we arrived he had wrested the boat off the car singlehanded.

Upriver, the sky was beginning to lighten as we rowed the slow stretch between the Walker and Early holes.

"Easy! Easy now." Bill cautioned as we neared the pool. "Fish were in the top end yesterday."

He lowered an anchor and I followed so we were both in position to cover the water. Some time passed without a strike or a fish showing. Then, some distance below us, in the deepest part of the hole a huge salmon erupted against the surface, breaking the mirrorlike reflection with ever-widening rings. We drifted down. Our anchors hit bottom at thirty feet and in the full light of dawn you could see them sitting down there on the ends of their ropes.

Shortly, Bill hooked a salmon that he played from his anchored boat. It was a smallish fish, no more than fifteen pounds and he gaffed it in the lip with a tiny hook of his own making. In the next few hours he caught half a dozen more, including one beautiful bright male over forty pounds.

"You using lead?" He finally said to me.

I nodded, knowing he was too.

"You must be going under them," he offered. "I've taken some of the lead out of my line in sections so I don't go too deep. Plastic sinks too slow and plain lead line too fast. Here, try this."

He tossed me a line wrapped around a piece of cardboard which I substituted for the one I was using. Lead-core line is often a necessity in fly-fishing for salmon but it is a specialized piece of equipment and difficult to manage.

Bill carries a variety that sink at different rates. Taking pieces of lead out in sections is only one of his inventions. In another case, he removed all the lead wire from a thirty-foot section and substituted .30 lead fuse wire to make a line that weighed close to eight hundred grains. The heaviest fly line on the standard scale weighs three hundred and fifty grains, so any less a caster than Schaadt cannot fish with "the cable." Some water on the Smith is so fast that only this big line will cut through it, and since Bill is the only one who has such a line and the only person who can cast it, there are places only he can fish.

With the borrowed line I soon had a strike and drifted over to the cliff to play the fish. Here, a rock projection formed a right angle to the current and the resulting swirl had dug a pocket more than ninety feet deep. As I played the salmon straight up and down, I could feel him going into underwater caves, sawing the line on sharp rock.

Finally the line snagged so I took the boat far back into the corner where it came free. When I got out on a tiny outcropping just large enough for my two feet, the boat drifted away leaving me stranded.

The morning sun slanted into the fantastic depths where I could see my salmon twisting far below. It looked about six inches long. As I worked him up he became a foot long, then two, three and finally close to four, wallowing at my feet. If I tried to bend forward my backside would hit the wall in back and I'd do a half gainer into the Smith. All I could do was reach sideways and grab. Then I was caught by my salmon.

"What the hell are you doing over there?" Bill called.

Knowing he'd have to help me, I was mortified. Asking Bill Schaadt to stop fishing was unthinkable but I couldn't move a muscle.

"Guess I'm stuck," I said.

"Be right over." He laughed.

He took the forty-five-pound fish into his boat with a powerful sweep and I toppled in beside it. We retrieved my boat and both started fishing again.

After a while he looked at me and said, "If you hook another one, take it to the beach."

Angling is perhaps wrongly called a sport for it is not precisely one at all, at least not in the competitive sense. There are many fishing contests and tournaments but these seem to be entirely beside the point. To compete against another angler is to do so once removed and always on an unequal basis. It may be that a certain stretching of the truth is one of angling's proper embellishments and that objectivity tends only to destroy the romance. What does it matter who the best fisherman is and how could this be determined if it did? Most anglers who place a high value on their activity are contemptuous of the competitive approach and look upon the "experts" with grave suspicion.

"Serious" angling attracts an inordinate number of boobs. The reason could be that it is entirely possible to become widely known as an authority strictly on the basis of fiction, luck or hearsay.

It may be accurate to say that if golf were to be likened to fishing, the hole would have to be a living thing with an appetite and a temperament that varied widely from green to green and course to course.

The golfer would then try to tempt the hole to accept his ball by perhaps alternately shooting a McGregor Tourney, Titleist or Dunlop Maxfli. It would often turn out that no matter how crafty the golfer, the hole might simply eye the ball suspiciously then sidle away. It would also frequently occur that a complete tyro dribbled a shot into the rough only to have the hole charge, root around in the underbrush and grab the ball, whereupon he would have shot a hole in one. And some holes might gain a reputation for being especially difficult, like the permit fish, and would be eagerly sought after by a certain class of golfer interested in aesthetics and severe hardship.

There are a lot of myths surrounding fly-fishing and its attendant difficulties. Surely the percentage of excellent casters among fly-fishermen is less than the same level of competence found in most other sports. Perhaps this is because the rewards are private. Put a few hundred grand on the line and no doubt some very cool hands would begin appearing at the casting tournaments.

The Golden Gate Angling and Casting Club in San Francisco is famous for having produced many great casters. I spent a lot of time there when I was younger and while my abilities never progressed much beyond being fairly competent, I did gain a very clear idea of what can and cannot be done with a fly rod. You cannot, for example, stand in the stern of a bonefish skiff and cast a tarpon fly a hundred feet into the wind. No matter who you are.

Bill Schaadt has more physical ability and co-ordination than anyone I've ever known. I'm often embarrassed to cast alongside him because he is so superior. Jon Tarantino, until his death, was considered by many to be the greatest distance fly-caster who ever lived. He was the only man clearly the equal of Bill Schaadt.

Schaadt's tackle is inexpensive and shabby. He· uses one-piece fiberglass rods fitted with rough thick handles and guides that are crudely lashed on with a bobbin. His equipment would send an Abercrombie & Fitch salesman scurrying for the rest room. In spite of this, everything Schaadt uses functions smoothly and is well balanced. There is no naïveté in its preparation or application.

Most well-known anglers have gained their notoriety by catching large fish. Schaadt has caught more big steelhead and salmon than any man who ever lived. Included is a fifty-six-pound king salmon, the largest ever landed on a fly, but this does not seem to be the criteria to best judge his merit as an angler. It is his over-all sense of understanding, deep love of the natural world, energetic effort and his style, which set him so clearly apart from his contemporaries.

"We're in the bucket!" Bill exclaimed, lacing another cast over the pool.

The intensity with which he fishes is inspiring. Bill began to eat his lunch one-handed. He'd cast, then in the several seconds it took for the line to sink, he'd take a quick bite out of a sandwich then set it down and retrieve the fly, cast again, then take another bite. I have never known him to fish less than from dawn to dark with no stops in between for food or conversation. Once he was fishing a run so wide he had to wade within two inches of the top of his chest-high waders and then make hundred-foot casts. Realizing this was far too strenuous to maintain for long, he went up to the car and brought down his sign painter's step ladder, which he then carried out to where he'd been wading. Then he simply climbed up on it and fished in comfort. And when he arises tomorrow or the next day, or next year, it will be with the same enthusiasm as twenty years ago. When he hooks a fish he often gets so excited he screams and yells so that fishermen nearby who don't know who he is often remark, "Boy, that must be the first one that guy ever caught."

Fishing slowed to a standstill under the brightness of midday but Bill did not think of taking a break. Instead, knowing salmon were still milling in the pool, he tied on a twenty-foot leader with a light tippet and a number-ten fly, hoping to get a take from the reticent fish. Strain your imagination and visualize this outrageous tackle behaving perfectly in the air, landing in an immaculate turnover with the nearly invisible fly extending itself to the end of that unlikely leader.

An hour of casting produced nothing. When I reeled in to eat lunch Schaadt threw me an accusing stare. He reeled in his line with blinding speed, wrenched his anchor up and began churning toward the corner.

"Sometimes they go back in here during the middle of the day," he said, surging across the pool. He backed up his boat against the cliff and tied it to a rock. I was not paying close attention as I ate my lunch.

Soon I became aware of something peculiar going on. Schaadt was making long casts but this didn't seem possible because his back was to a high cliff. I began watching intently. I could see violent slashing motions, water flying everywhere, then an incredible drive that seemed to lift the line miraculously into the air, sending it out a full eighty feet. He was making a kind of roll cast. Every fly-fisherman learns to roll cast as a means of bringing a sunken line to the surface or simply making a very short throw when there is no room for a backcast.

This was something far beyond that. Bill had discovered a method of building line speed with a series of circular lifts while keeping a precise amount of drag on the front of the line, which remained in the water. On the final lift, line was allowed to sag slightly to the rear so that the double haul could be used. Ultimately, a tremendous drive forward and a strong pull with the left hand lifted the shooting head cleanly into the air, putting a point on it to deliver a fishable cast.

I've practiced this in the years since that day on the Smith, never fully admitting to Bill I couldn't manage what to him was a routine cast. A dozen years later, I get about two thirds of his distance and I've not met a single other fisherman who's mastered the cast either.

After the war people began fishing more and more so naturally the sport developed. Schaadt moved to the Russian River from San Francisco in the mid-forties and took a job in a garage in Guerneville. He loved the river so much he bought a lot in the tiny town of Monte Rio and built himself a place. Unable to tolerate the restrictions of regular employment, Bill discovered sign painting and became the only one in the area.

In a resort community all effort is directed at the summer trade, so Bill would be busy during the late spring and summer painting signs, and have the fall and winter off. Nothing could be more perfect because this is the time when fishing is best.

When I first met Schaadt I was interested in learning the sign painter's trade and spent a lot of time at a sign shop near my home. I quickly realized I didn't have the hand or the patience for the work but I could never tire of watching Bill. His natural ability gives his work swing, as it's called in the business, which means that his letters and words move well together.

Suppose he were painting the words REAL ESTATE, the final effect of which was to be a casually vigorous script. Using a wide, square-tipped sable brush called a greyhound, Schaadt might very well cut in the letter E in the word REAL first.

Then he might do the L. From there he might go to the last E in ESTATE while next would come the middle T of the same word.

Until the last few minutes the whole thing might more closely resemble an abstract expressionist painting than a sign. The reason for working this way is that the air or space between the letters is every bit as important as the letters themselves. Then, too, in large script the letters do become more or less abstract shapes. Many signwriters work this way but few with Schaadt's flair.

He was raised in San Francisco and briefly attended the California School of Fine Art (now the San Francisco Art Institute) but lost patience with it. Once he showed me a sketch book with a few nudes he'd done that appeared to be studies after Reubens, but Bill seemed to have little interest in them.

Schaadt is not the quiet, contemplative type. His day is filled with a multiplicity of projects. His cars alone are more than an ordinary person could handle. He always seems to have about three that run and at least that many which don't. These are usually in the process of being rebuilt.

Similarly six or eight boats are stored on the rack just inside the yard. A certain number of these need annual attention and there is inevitably some newly acquired craft being rebuilt or fiberglassed.

The sewing machine is one of Bill's most frequently used tools. He remakes all the upholstery for the cars, sews leather, awnings, tarps, and he keeps his own extensive wardrobe in tidy repair. It is typical that while doing some mending, Bill will get carried away and begin embroidering designs on some garment or other. And, stitched somewhere, you can find his name and perhaps a fly or a leaping trout.

A few years ago he built a very handsome and serviceable workshop in his yard. As might be expected, he split the redwood shakes that cover it himself, starting out with a large tree.

Inside the shop, leaning against the walls as well as tied to all the rafters, are an astonishing number of bicycles. There are motorcycles and scooters too, some of which Schaadt built. He is a bike freak, selling and trading them around town and he can sometimes be prevailed upon to repair them.

Once he and I were standing around his yard talking when there was a clatter of young voices outside the gate.

"Schaadt!" a tiny voice called out.

"Hey, Schaadt!"

"Shhhh," Bill whispered to me. "Quiet, they'll beat it."

"Schaadt! Hey, Schaadt! Jimmy's bike broke on the front. Can you fix it, Schaadt?"

"Damn!" Bill uttered. He swung open the gate and half a dozen kids swarmed in. He was the picture of friendliness and obviously loved fixing the bike. He worked hard for fifteen or twenty minutes until the trouble was straightened out and the kids rode off.

"Damn kids," he said.

The one constant factor in coastal fishing in California over the last quarter of a century is Bill Schaadt. He has not missed a single fall or winter's day at it in that time.

He used to go to the Klamath in September and stay until the lower Eel got good, and when that was rained out he'd go back home and fish the Russian all winter. But the California fishery is almost a thing of the past. In 1956 Schaadt landed between eight hundred and nine hundred steelhead in the Russian River. Fishing the same number of hours today he would feel lucky to catch twenty.

The only prime stream left in California is the Smith River in the extreme northwestern corner of the state. It remains undammed, its drainages have not yet been too badly spoiled by logging and it runs an exceptionally large strain of both steelhead and salmon. Today, Schaadt confines almost all of his fishing to this river. He takes his small trailer up there from Monte Rio early in the fall and stays until the heavy winter rains make fishing impossible.

His knowledge of the river and especially of its salmon has reached the profound. Much of what he does is so obscure that only the most advanced fisherman could see it. On the other hand, the essential thing he does is so simple it is inclined to be overlooked: he fishes the longest and the hardest.

Not only that, but he fishes the longest and the hardest in the best place. One verity in this type of fishing is that there is almost always a best place. Each hole has its "bucket" and when fish are holding they will favor one hole or another. It is axiomatic that Schaadt will always be in the best place in the best hole.

This is one reason many people don't like Bill. He does not view the situation democratically. He feels that if he's willing to get up every morning at three-thirty in order to plant his feet or his boat in the precise location of his choosing, then he's damn well entitled to fish there forever. As long as he doesn't leave temporarily.

One day last fall a group of us were fishing a certain pool. You could get your fly into the salmon from any one of half a dozen positions but there was one prime spot which Bill was in every day.

Since people gravitate toward him, the pool was becoming more and more crowded and Bill was having to get up earlier and earlier each morning to be sure of fishing exactly where he wanted.

One morning he got down to the river about four-thirty to find a spin fisherman in his spot. The man had been watching the day before and had decided Bill was in the best place, so he'd got up unreasonably early (more unreasonably early than Bill in this case) and arrived at the river first.

All morning Bill worked around this fellow, who was no Philadelphia lawyer as a fisherman. The rest of us could see the frustration building as the spin fisherman flung his bait fecklessly time and again into the choicest water. After some hours he finally hooked a salmon which took him several hundred yards down the pool. Meantime Bill slid into his spot to get in a little fishing.

Of course, after landing his fish the spinner came back and stood for a moment behind Bill.

"Excuse me, sir," he said, "but I think that's my spot."

"Yes," Bill said through gritted teeth. "It is your spot and I'm moving because you were here first."

All our attention was on the scene as Bill continued to address the fisherman.

"But let me tell you something," Bill went on. "In order for you to ever get this spot again, you're going to have to get down here at midnight!"

The man's eyes widened.

"And another thing, if you leave this spot today to go and eat lunch, when you come back you're going to be out. Do you understand that? OUT! Out, out, out, out, out, out, out, out, out, out, out, out!" And he gave the astonished man about fifty outs all the while gesturing like an umpire signaling a player safe at first.

31

A silver dusk was settling on the Early Hole. I was weary from a long and fishless afternoon. My casting had become more like half-hearted throwing and I'd have been glad to quit right then.

Bill stood eagerly in the stern of his boat making the same long, graceful casts he had in the first light of dawn. If anything, he was more intense than earlier. I think toward evening he becomes impatient with nature because the night shuts things down and he has to go home and sleep awhile before he can fish some more. When we were in the Florida Keys together where much fishing is done at night, he fished all day and all night, catching little fifteen-minute naps like Thomas Edison used to do when he was working in his laboratory.

"It's grab time," Bill stated with perfectly unwarranted enthusiasm.

We fished until it was absolutely pitch dark and the salmon started to roll, but we caught nothing. I reeled in, pulled my anchor and started rowing back.

Bill took his regular fly off replacing it with a large black one, made a cast, then pulled his anchor and began rowing slowly out of the pool.

"Got one!" I heard him yell somewhere in the dark. I rowed back and he was all excited and laughing.

"Thought I'd troll out of the hole," he said. "You see, it's never too late!"

Chapter Two

A CERTAIN MOMENT

The fisherman's day began before daylight. Roads were lightly iced where water seeped from a rain earlier in the week and a dense tule fog hugged the valleys. Eaves were white with frost in San Anselmo and the vague predawn light showed Fairfax was utterly deserted. The landscape surrounding the rest of the drive lay pristinely beneath a silver mantle;

White's Hill, San Geronimo Valley, Samuel P. Taylor State Park and finally, Tocaloma and the Olema Grade, giving rise at its crest to the full sweep of Inverness Ridge and Tomales Bay where the fisherman was going after striped bass.

Near the town of Point Reyes Station the road branched left and at White House Pool steelhead fishermen were beginning to gather. Beyond Inverness Park, past Willow Point, the road skirted the bay and the angler pulled onto a wide shoulder. As he stepped from the car and walked to the water's edge, ice and frost crunched beneath his feet.

Dawn was breaking and the brittle air hung still, with the mingled scents of the marsh and wet farmland in it. Except for the distant rumble of the sea at Point Reyes and the intermittent call of a mallard out on the nearby moor, it was silent. Over the water itself a light mist spiraled gently toward a clear azure sky in which the morning star was quickly dimming.

A light eight-foot boat soon sat ready at the water's edge. There had been a choice in launching locations: here, to fish the morning high water without having to row for an hour right at the start, or down at the Golden Hind dock which would be convenient, necessary actually, later on the minus tide when it was time to come in. The fisherman chose the former, deciding to come ashore at the yacht club or wherever he could, then walk back to his car.

The rod was strung, a fly which at the moment appealed, tied on, then the tackle set on the seat, tip over the stern. In minutes the trim *El Toro* was rhythmically disturbing the surface trailing a wake of foam and bubbles. Ahead, behind his back, the fisherman heard the cries of water birds as they took flight.

Choosing what he thought was a likely area on the flooding

water, he drifted with the tide, casting at random. An hour passed. There were baitfish everywhere and when the sun had risen well in the sky several little Bonaparte's gulls started fluttering and diving to feed. Several times bass surfaced but on so widely divergent tangents that it was useless to try and discover a pattern. All he could do was fish the vicinity and hope.

The day grew to be one of those sublime moments that winter sometimes offers as counterpoint. The cloudless air was pure, almost fragile, the temperature hovering in the sixties. Earlier it had been cold enough for wispy sheets of ice to form against the shoreline but now the sun was at its winter zenith.

The angler had further reasons for remaining confident even though the first enthusiasm of morning had long waned. In previous weeks he'd caught enough fish so that as the hour or tide changed he could always recall a success during conditions similar to almost any present moment.

Nearby, a flock of bluebill circled, set their wings and alighted. The myriad bay ducks—scoter, mud hen, bufflehead, goldeneye, ruddy—were moving continually and to distinguish between their rings and one made by a surfacing bass was impossible. Overhead great V's of pintail whistled and once, very high, geese.

Because of the low water at sundown, the tide, which had started to fall at noon now ran rapidly. The wind blowing against it caused the boat to drift at an angle across the bay rather than with either wind or tide alone. By casting to one side then the other as the boat moved, great swaths of water were probed. Assuming an average cast to be seventy feet, each pass ate up a ribbon of territory a hundred and forty feet wide. Using a floating head and dark streamer, the angler confined his drifts to areas no more than four feet deep as the stripers seemed to maintain this level as the tide fell.

All during the afternoon he found nothing. Later, an occasional cast failed to straighten causing irritation. The flats had not produced as they should have and the tide was steadily drying them up. As he turned to watch a backcast fling spray into the afternoon sun he knew it was time to move. The sun was lowering against the peninsula and soon the short twilight of winter would gather.

The angler had thought of the oyster bed during the morning but not especially as the last resort it had now become. He'd fully expected to catch fish at intervals throughout the outgoing tide then move there on the low water. He knew the cove near the fence held bass on a minus tide when the broad expanse to the south was completely dry.

As he rowed from near the yacht club over to Millerton Point, the breeze died and the air became icy still as it had been at dawn. The many birds so obvious earlier could no longer be seen clearly and the shoreline was becoming indistinct behind a bluish haze through which only an occasional light sparkled. The earth was immersing itself into the pearly liquid of dusk. Exposed shoreline crackled and Inverness Ridge loomed blackly, its forest of ancient pine standing in sharp contrast to the sensual, easy slopes of the hills to the east. In the distance a chain saw whined, and behind the town thin columns of smoke eased skyward as night began to fall.

Nearby, the oyster fence lent a certain definition to the otherwise abstruse basin the angler hoped to fish. Like sentinels, the long row of slender eucalyptus poles stretched away to the north guarding vulnerable crustaceans against the appetites of the many large bat rays that inhabit the bay. In places the fence suffered the disrepair of time, which seemed to give it a particular attraction.

Nearing the stakes, the fisherman drew his oars carefully back through the locks after a final stroke which sent the little boat surging forward. On the glassy water the boat drifted slowly, then stopped. Picking up the fly rod, he took the slender bucktail from the cork grip, dropped it over and watched it vanish into the green, past the faintly reflected rose sky.

Downward thrusts lay a pattern of loose monofilament in the boat followed by a tentative false cast before the rod hissed a lean delivery eighty feet toward the fence. As the fly settled he imagined its descent into dimness to be as he remembered it alongside the boat. The next cast straightened several yards to the right of the first to begin a radius that would eventually strike all the water.

When nearly half the second cast was recovered, there was a boil behind the fly. Had the surface not been still it would have gone unnoticed and, in fact, so subtle was this evidence of a missed strike that it was at once undeniable and unbelievable. The fish had stayed deep: cruising, it had arched beneath the bait, turning in an attempted take to make the surface well up in a restrained convulsion.

The disturbance had scarcely dissipated when the next cast was formed of slow, mannered loops which slid smoothly forward, back, then far forward in a point that carried line and fly again to the bass. Sensing the lethargy of the season, the angler slowed the retrieve, inducing several more passes. Near the boat the line tightened but when he struck there was nothing.

It seemed inevitable that the line should pull up again as it had before, only this time his response was met with solid resistance and the long rod curved fully, its tip held low. Unbalanced momentarily, he saw at the top of his vision the water open and churn then bulge in an uncertain way as the fish moved off. Loose line, which had been coiled haplessly in the boat, snapped against the guides until it was taut from the reel that then released it in spasms as the bass surged away.

Fifty yards of line hummed under the strain while the rod told of the fish's pulsing attempts to free itself as it circled widely. The boat turned and moved with the bass, but even so, recovered line was soon lost. This was the linear fight of the shallows. When the fish ran, the rod plunged, then came back as the reel gave line until the run ceased, then the rod went down again as line went back onto the spool.

Soon the bass was thrashing nearby, turning, boring down and away. It seemed so dark, its green back glistening, its stripes so sharply defined. Once it thrust its tail, sending a crescent of water over the angler.

In a moment the striper lay motionless off the transom. But it dived beneath the boat and then away in a tight arc which brought it to the surface again a few feet out. This time in a quick succession of moves, the fisherman took the leader in his left hand, set the rod down, grabbed the hook shank with his right, clamped his left on the fish's jaw and, using this paralyzing grip lifted twenty pounds of striped bass over the gunwale.

There was still enough light in the afterglow to have fished longer but he didn't. It had been a difficult day and this was its proper conclusion. He snipped the leader and wound in the line.

The sky was pale lemon toward the ocean and a light was on at the oyster company. Stars were coming out strongly above, and Inverness glimmered from across the bay as the angler started the long row back. Settling into the rhythm of it, he glanced behind him to look at the fish but saw instead, a three-quarter moon lifting importantly over the gently rolling hills in the east.

In the magic, almost colorless light, the bass glinted from the bow, its lifeless form stretched over coils of rope. He felt mutely accused and melancholy over this complicated yet unplanned death. The perfect eye, which moments earlier had guided the fatal chase, no longer saw. But the decision was final, the memory forever etched; he had done as he would do, and in the morning would perhaps arise again before dawn and begin another day of fishing.

Chapter Three

HARD AS A ROCK

As is often the case during summer, the northern California coast was fogbound. From the vast windows of the house where I was staying I could barely see any of it. For example, I couldn't see across the inlet to where the quaint town of Mendocino inhabited its mesa, a town so patently picturesque it was almost a relief not to be able to see it.

I was an anonymous painter behind plate glass. This was important at the moment because Mendocino is one of the artiest art colonies on the coast. There could be guilt by association: the county was dark with arts and crafts, decorated Volkswagen buses, inept pottery, macramé and embarrassing paintings. I was here to go fishing.

My friend Harry had just gotten back from an afternoon of gathering mussels and abalone. He had been with his friend Charlie, a writer, who considered it imperative that a part of each day be spent trying to catch *something*. Since there would be three of us going rockfishing the next day, Charlie was careful to save the abalone guts for bait.

"I won't need any," I said. "I'm going to use flies."

Charlie scanned me for signs of brain damage. Without resolving the question, he put all the guts into a big plastic bag.

"*We're going to need lots of bait!*" he stated, with a concerned glance at me.

Charlie was not an early riser so Harry and I had to amuse ourselves throughout the morning. Harry was a sculptor and an exhibition of his work was at one of the galleries so we went over to see it. The gallery was an old shed which had been whitewashed inside and out. The lady who ran it had graying hair and wore faded blue jeans and a tasteful handmade shawl. This was standard.

"They never sell a damn thing," Harry remarked after we left. "Were you kidding?" he asked me.

"About what?"

"You can't use flies in the ocean can you?"

"Sure, you'll see."

There was a certain broad headland where Harry and Charlie had permission to fish. It was a grassy meadow with

pine and cypress trees along its north side ending abruptly at
a rocky drop to the ocean. Fog hugged it closely and the still
air was damp and rich with sea smells.

Harry had a long bamboo pole with a short length of wire
tied to the end of it. He was going "poke-poling." This is
where you poke the pole with its short wire leader and baited
hook down into crevices in the rock. He would catch mostly
eels and cabezon this way.

Charlie had an ordinary stout fishing rod and a big Penn
reel. He used Bull Durhum bags filled with sand for sinkers
because they didn't snag so easily on the irregular bottom.
And if he did lose one, it didn't matter because he had a lot
more.

I had my fly rod and some concern was expressed over this.
Charlie was anxious to arrange a wager before we began. He
renewed his offer of abalone guts.

In truth, Charlie's interest in fishing was not entirely a matter of catching fish. One of the reasons was that he didn't
catch many, but the real reason was that for him, time spent
fishing was time spent thinking. When he was sitting out
there he turned over ideas, invented characters, built plots
and considered Beethoven's late string quartets. Inadvert-
ently, I was going to ruin this for him.

"Catch many black snappers?" I asked.

"Once in a while. Wish I'd catch more."

"I'll get you a sackful," I promised with a smile.

"Ha!"

Years ago I might have said, Ha! In fact, I did say, Ha! once
about fifteen years ago. The thing is I didn't say it out loud so
I didn't have to eat it afterward. I was with Bill Schaadt
careening up coast Highway 1 in an old Plymouth, past Fort
Ross to a place just south of Salt Point, which he called the

Rope Hole. It was called the Rope Hole because it was so far down and so steep you had to climb down and up a rope to get there and back.

We were just getting the hang of fly line with lead wire in it, which was the main ingredient for successful rockfishing. This kind of line cut through the wash to where the fish were. We learned any kind of fly worked—old steelhead flies for example. It was easier though just to tie an orange feather on a hook.

That day Bill and I caught our limit of snappers, which was twenty apiece. I had cause to regret this on our way back up the rope. It was perhaps as close as I've ever come to cardiac arrest.

We did a great deal of fly-fishing for snappers after that. Once, we foolishly launched a skiff and went out the mouth of the Russian River. We caught snappers all right, but were lucky to get back through the breakers. We fished at Salt Point, Fort Ross and a hundred other nameless places in between. Later, I fished up and down the Oregon and Washington coasts. So I was a seasoned rockfisherman, a fact that Charlie hardly suspected.

Charlie was at a spot where a deep crevice cut back between two high slabs of rock. Here the surf surged in and out with mesmeric regularity, alternately revealing and hiding the bottom beneath lime-green foam. He caught an exotic rainbow perch on his first throw and was overly matter-of-fact about it.

"Bait?" he offered, with an upraised eyebrow.

Nearby, I found a deep hole ringed with kelp. Long casts are built into the lead line and with the help of an elevated position I dropped one about a hundred feet out. Charlie's eyes widened. He had never seen anything like it. He wondered no doubt what this painter, this, this . . . mere dauber was up to. He did not suspect that without even stepping lightly into a phone booth that I—in the presence of catchable quarry—could rearrange my chromosomes into a facsimile of the mythical angler, Reeline Waderfly, who stopped at nothing in his neurotic quest for fish. And who was to sire the seeds of Charlie's imminent discontent.

A three-pound snapper took the fly immediately. The next cast was another one and so on until the burlap sack had been mercilessly filled. Meanwhile, Charlie sat hunched over his inert fishing rod.

When Harry rejoined us he was soaking wet and shivering. He had gotten way out on a reef and a big roller simply lifted him off, carried him out, then swept him back, depositing him again on the reef. He'd lost his sack of fish and had some pretty bad scrapes from sharp rock and mussels. It was time to go home.

Charlie was not the least bit glum. At the house he cheerfully assaulted a bottle of sauterne with a gleam in his eye which became a glaze at precisely the same rate as the level of liquid dropped.

I explained to him that the snappers liked to stay fairly high in the water, especially near kelp, and that he caught so few because his bait was on the bottom. I suggested he try a bobber but he wasn't listening. He reminded me of Mr. Toad seeing his first motor car.

"This is it," he said, "the miracle method!"

Sometime later I met Harry in San Francisco. He told me Charlie had gone up to Fort Bragg and bought a fly rod and reel on sale at one of the drug stores. He couldn't find any of that special line so he just got whatever they had.

"He's not the same," Harry went on. "He goes down every

day and flails around on the rocks. There's no one to show him what to do and people think he's gone around the bend. Most of the time he's got his hook stuck in the kelp or on a rock or bush. Either that or in the seat of his pants. I think he can only throw it out about ten feet at best, which frustrates him so he comes home all on edge instead of soothed and relaxed like he used to. And he risks his life trying to get too far out on the reef because he knows he can't cast out to where the fish are. He doesn't even talk about Beethoven any more."

"Has he caught anything?"

"Not yet."

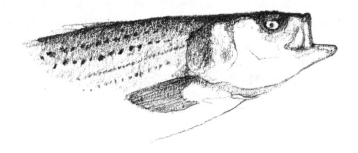

Chapter Four

NO WIND IN THE WILLOWS

Outside a blizzard is raging. The familiar edges that normally define my yard, its fences, woodpile and barns, have long vanished beneath the snow. My house, the last on an unpaved road among aspen and pine forests along the northwestern perimeter of Montana's vast Absaroka wilderness, is well on its way toward becoming a smallish speck on the surface of a preposterous marshmallow.

No Wind in the Willows

Unable to go out, perhaps I will simply sit, reminisce and revisit. A word recurs, an idea, insisting itself upon the situation: *remoteness.* I moved to the Big Sky Country to get it. As an angler reflecting upon the fabric of American sport afield, I recognized the essential thread to be a romance with far places. In short, I'd identified the Mainstream and wanted in.

Early on, my fishing days were spent in a northern California cabin snugged against the hillside beneath stands of redwood. On a bookshelf beside its fireplace was a pile of old magazines, sporting journals mostly, and some outdated tackle catalogues. It seemed fishing was more plain and intimate then. For example, the invocation, "Take a boy fishing!" required but a few Bass-O-Renos and perhaps a small outboard motor, called a "kicker," for immediate implementation.

This pastiche of allusions then, was rife with visions of adventure in which the canoe loomed large as a vehicle of escape. A guide, invariably of French descent, dressed appropriately in a red- and black-checked wool shirt, took us to lakes and rivers teeming with unusually large brook trout or northern pike somewhere in the vastness of the Candian outback.

Portage! How much more a vision of unsoiled landscape this word promises than . . . ecology.

But before I founder completely in fatuous recall, it occurs that until very recently, among the hundred-odd thousand words placed by the Oxford Unabridged at my disposal, the adjective least correct as a predicate to my own angling past is *remote.*

San Francisco Bay: It is four-thirty in the morning on June 21, 1966. I am later than planned because of the time it took to clear myself with the policeman who pulled me over in San Anselmo for "suspicious behavior." Was it the generally fishy odor about the car which, in the end, convinced the law of my salient innocence? I don't know. In any case, we had parted amicably.

Now I am parking the car near a maintenance station on the Marin County end of the Richmond-San Rafael Bridge. I expect to be joined soon by an acquaintance but since he hasn't arrived I decide to walk out to the bridge itself for a quick preview.

On the way, rats scurry for cover behind a shabby row of shrubs. These would not be your big Norways, the kind you might see in the tropics sitting boldly in a palm while you sip your rum and tonic on the veranda below. No, the pusillanimous little rodents that people my morning are inclined to cower behind slimy rocks near the freeway, struggling on an equal footing with Marfak for control of the last strands of seaweed, or waiting in crevices for the next high tide.

I brush past the PEDESTRIANS PROHIBITED sign, jump the low guard rail and trot to the second light post. There is no visible traffic but from the north I hear a diesel truck shift down just before the crest that will bring him into view and then onto the bridge approach. He will be doing seventy when he reaches me so I hook one leg over the railing, grip the light standard and try to become inconspicuous. I would rather not be sucked under the rear wheels of a truck and trailer full of rutabagas. He goes by with a blast and the bridge vibrates ominously as I watch his lights diminish toward Richmond.

I run out to the next light and look down. As I'd hoped, half a dozen dark forms are finning in the shadow beneath the bridge. I am especially excited by the largest, which is a striped bass upward of thirty pounds. To my right, a pod of smelt moves near on a tangent certain to prompt an attack. The little fish are attracted by the brilliant light overhead. In their lack of purpose they seem ephemeral, like a translucent curtain quivering near a window, while the heavy predators lurking in the dark are deliberate and potent. In a moment the black shapes explode outward, sending the smelt showering away in a radius of flashing bodies.

Satisfied, I turn back toward the approach in time to see the California Highway Patrol car coming at me, its nose down under heavy braking.

"What are you doing out here, buddy?"

"Going fishing soon as it's legal time."

"Is that your car parked back at the maintenance building?"

"Yes."

"Well it's illegally parked. Better move it. Now get going and don't walk out here any more."

On my way to the car I see the patrolman who'd questioned me get out and look over the railing. Then the amber light is flashing and the driver is out too. Together they lean over the side, pointing.

I recognize Frank's blue sedan come down the off ramp and turn south. When I reach him he is untying his boat and I begin to do the same. In a few seconds we will have them in the water.

In order to launch we must trespass. The land belongs to the state of California and although I've never been verbally warned off, any number of KEEP OUT signs are posted.

For about eight years I kept a boat chained and locked

behind a large sign reading CABLE CROSSING. Once a year they would repaint this sign getting white paint on the chain.

Some yards away in a square blockhouse belonging to San Quentin Penitentiary, trustees worked during the day. Each season they planted a handsome little vegetable garden which I was careful never to disturb.

I often talked to one convict in particular. After fishing it would take some minutes to put the boat behind the sign and then carry everything else up to the car. He would call a greeting and I'd perhaps comment on the progress in the garden. Then he'd ask, always rather plaintively, about the fishing. He said he liked to go fishing before he got "inside."

One December we had a severe storm, accompanied by especially high tides. Afterward, I went over to check the boat and all that was left was the chain. I was poking around the beach when I heard my friend's voice.

"Looking for your boat?"

"Guess it's gone," I replied sadly.

"No, I saw it break loose and caught it. Then I dragged it up there." He said, "Only thing I couldn't find was the seat."

Beyond the garden I could see the trim little *El Toro* upside down on a pair of two by fours.

In recent years there have been no inmates at the blockhouse and the garden lies fallow beneath wild anise. In a sense this has meant more license to trespass but I stopped keeping a boat behind the sign when I knew there would be no trustees to look after it.

It is a windless, overcast morning. Sunrise, such as it will be, is in an hour but the eastern horizon over San Pablo Bay is still dark. Bursts of flame glow against a cloudy ceiling above Point Molate, tangible evidence that behind the latter's headlands lies the Standard Oil Company of California's research center, in a bitter sense, petroleum's ode to the cubists with its sprawl of cylinders, cones and rectangles.

At Point San Quentin, the flaring fires have become a familiar greeting like the dew on a chokecherry bush that starts off the trout fisherman's day in the Rockies.

"Did you look?" Frank asks.

"They're there."

We row around the tilted bow of a derelict tugboat, then past rotted pilings left from the ferryboat days. Over on the approach a yellow bridge patrol truck moves slowly, flashing its warning lights. Switching on a spotlight, the driver scans the water, catching sight of Frank and me. Then the light is off and the truck starts toward the toll plaza.

Unseen overhead, a black-crowned night hawk rasps its singularly forlorn call.

The smell of an institutional breakfast wafts unappetizingly across the water from San Quentin, an odor not unlike that of a cow barn in winter. No croissants and chilled grapefruit sections this morning, to be sure.

There is a fast tide and we must row smartly to pass beneath the bridge, where it is always dank and dripping. Sounds are magnified and echoed, especially that of wavelets slapping against pilings. Reflected light plays on the girders overhead, and just before we emerge I see several bass hovering at the edge, but Frank rows into the dark while I decide to try a few casts at the first light. The piling directly beneath the lamp attracts my attention so I drop the large bucktail fly where the current will swing it into the shadows.

Instantly there is a take and I set the hook twice. This is always the moment when you wonder if the bass will go under the bridge and break off on a sharp barnacle. But I've learned that initial light pressure generally encourages them to dive toward the boat.

Now my bass pulls around into the dark, and I try to gauge its size. It is, if nothing else, a stubborn fish that resolutely resists all the strain I can manage on a fifteen-pound tippet. Eventually, however, I land it and mentally record a weight slightly above twenty pounds.

Frank is anchored under the third light, where I see angular splashes as fish erupt under a school of bait.

It was Walt Mullen who showed me the bridge and how to fish it shortly after it was built. When we first met I was sixteen and he was more than eighty. Coincidentally, Walt had taken my father fishing and hunting back in the twenties when the latter was going to Stanford.

Mullen was an old sign painter, wiry and spry, surely no more than a hundred pounds soaking wet. I wanted to learn the sign business so I'd hang around his shop. But my patience proved short and my business acumen entirely non-existent so we always ended up talking about fishing. He loved it more than anyone I'd ever met. In the front pocket of his coveralls he always had a tide book, dog-eared and paint-smeared.

"See here," he said one day, pointing out the numerals. "There's a good tide in three days. If the water's clear and it's not too windy, I'll take you out to the bridge."

At that point my own experience was primarily academic insofar as fly-casting for striped bass was concerned. Walt didn't fly-fish but he knew instinctively I would catch fish on the streamers I showed him.

I'd read about certain pioneer anglers on the East Coast who caught striped bass by fly-fishing. I knew also that Joe

Brooks, the noted Virginian, was much interested in stripers and that he caught one of twenty-nine pounds six ounces in 1948 out of Coos Bay, Oregon. This fish was acknowledged as the fly-rod record.

For several years Walt and I fished together regularly. Then I married and became too busy and he closed his shop, moving the business to another county.

Occasionally I'd see him at the bridge. His eyes were failing and he didn't trust himself in a boat any more so he'd cast from the rocks, often a futile gesture since fish rarely fed close to shore.

One windy, choppy evening Bill Schaadt and I were in our boat at the third light.

"Look." Bill pointed.

On the bridge, hunched against the railing, oblivious to speeding traffic and thoroughly unable to distinguish Bill or me, was Walt clutching an enormous spinning rod. Cocking it back, he used it to drive his lure in a trajectory which carried it over a school of bass I'm sure he never saw. His face was locked in an expression of determination that did not make him look any less like an angling Ichabod Crane.

"Boy," Bill said, "now there's a guy who likes to fish!"

Then as we'd hoped and anticipated, Walt hooked a striper whereupon he stalked grimly back to the rocks and landed it.

Several years passed during which time I did not see Walt Mullen. Then one cold spring morning I was out at the bridge alone. To avoid the noisome mob of trollers, with whom the bridge had become a favorite haunt, I'd begun going at odd hours and poorish tides. When it grew light I saw a figure on the rocks, casting. Walt! Excitedly I drew up my anchor and rowed in, circling widely so I wouldn't spoil anything. Close in, I turned but could no longer see anyone.

Going ashore, I called out with no response. I looked under the bridge and finally crossed the freeway to search the other side. There was no one. I felt a deep sense of loss, an uneasy melancholy. I went home.

Later I found out Walt had died earlier that spring.

I row around behind Frank. The bass are there and I see the heavy swirls as they feed.

Traffic on the bridge is picking up. Early commuters. They are too low in their cars to see us but the truck drivers give a wave or short blast of the horn. It is getting light, a gray dawn that I imagine could be heavily depressing to a man looking forward to eight hours on the production line.

"The coldest winter I ever spent," wrote someone, "was a summer in San Francisco." I wonder momentarily if this, in part, explains the high suicide rate and high alcohol intake for which the City on the Bay is known.

We are virtually within sight of well over a million people, yet alone. We are perhaps, out of step, ill placed and ill timed, in a sphere where cogs must mesh and all parts syncopate to keep the system running smoothly. Even within the framework of angling as a popular endeavor, our methods are archaic: fly rods and rowboats. But we are touching something unrestricted, wild and arcane, beyond the reach of those who carefully maintain one-dimensional lives. There is, I tell myself, someone in the city nearby whose one contact today with unreconstructed nature will be to step into a diminutive pile of poodle excrement.

When I looked into the mirror during the late fifties I saw a striped-bass fisherman who often imagined, wrongly, that he was doing something remarkable and unique.

At the time an old gent by the name of Ellis Springer was pier keeper for the Marin Rod and Gun Club, which was situated only a few feet from the bridge. He let me use the club's launching ramp, dock and fish-cleaning table even though I was not a member.

Ellis was never seen without a light-blue captain's hat and stubby cigar. He talked often of the days he'd spent in the Spanish-American War but his manner of speech was so unique that you could understand nothing of what he said. I didn't think he knew what fly-fishing was and wanting to let him in on my little discovery, I gave a demonstration one day off the dock. He looked properly astonished and when I showed him my flies, he became incoherently excited, exclaiming, "Yeeehhh! Hoopty poopty! Hoopty poopty!"

These exclamations became a permanent part of all subsequent conversations.

"Hi, Springer."

"Eeeeehhh! Hoopty poopty!"

I used to carry fish around in the back of my car the way other kids my age carried a six pack of Country Club. I'd show Ellis and he'd become truly frantic.

"Yeeeehhh! Hoopty poopty! Hoopty poopty!"

Gradually I became aware of the fact he called everything that was not strictly a sardine fillet a hoopty poopty.

Frank hooks a bass. I put my anchor down out of his way but still close enough to reach the school. I see two powerful boils and cast the bulky fly on a slow loop toward the swirl closest to a piling. I overshoot so the fly tinks against the bridge hanging momentarily between the rail and roadway, then as it flutters downward I see the number 9 stenciled above on an abutment.

The take is authoritative and my response lifts the clearly visible fly line from the water, curving it abruptly to the left as a sheet of droplets limns the fish's first long run. It is not a frenetic contest as the striper stays deep, far from the boat. But I am not inclined to carry out these contests gently and soon have the fish nearby. Once, glowering, he shoots away beneath a crescent of spray only to be turned in a verticle wallow. After all, nothing in their lives really prepares a fish to deal with the relentless affixation of being hooked.

Oddly, I am reminded of how Walt Mullen described playing a fish. "Then it fooled around and fooled around," he would say. And that is exactly it.

In the boat the fish is big.

"It's more than twenty-five," I say to Frank.

Earlier we had discussed a twenty-five-pound striper caught accidentally by a fly-fisherman in the Russian River. It seemed more appropriate that a fish taken by design should receive top honors for the season. Naturally, we both expressed the hope that one of us would catch such a fish.

Back at the beach we lay three large bass in front of the sign that reads CABLE CROSSING.

"That one's bigger than the one I caught last season," says Frank.

Getting his Polaroid camera, he takes a picture of me holding the fish, which comes out a minute later looking distant and journalistic. Then after promising to call him as soon as I get the thing weighed, I head for San Rafael and he goes off to work in San Francisco.

Later, I call.

"It's big isn't it?" Frank asks right away. "I've been looking at this snapshot all morning."

"Yes. Thirty-six pounds six ounces."

The record Joe Brooks had held for eighteen years was broken. When I got to know Joe he would always introduce me as "a great salt-water fisherman," which was embarrassing because while he was alive he was so clearly one of the greatest. Now others have caught bigger bass, eliminating my personal stake in the matter. It is a relief to be reminded that competition in angling is entirely beside the point and that I'm simply an angler of average persuasion and ability who happened to cast a fly near a large, hungry fish one morning.

Besides, there are too many other things to think about, like a certain broad shovel on the proch. I finished all the Jack Daniel's last night and this morning we are hopelessly snowed in.

Chapter Five

WADING FOR GODOT

Everything in nature is essentially inscrutable and certain elements seem to imply through a series of apexes the numinous structure hidden beneath. The grizzly may be a more public example say, than the peregrine falcon, of ostensible vulnerability. Its independence actually, requiring such rigorous maintenance that man's presence, let alone any distant hint of domesticity can be enough to reduce the animal to extinction or else drive him more deeply into what unfrequented wilderness may be left.

It seems feasible to apply a similar principle geographically as in the instance of Michigan's Upper Peninsula, where vast stands of white pine are gone and rivers are now barren of the delicate grayling. California, too, once the most abundant land in America, has suffered a mutation of its external face which surpasses the tragic. Its grizzly is extinct, now simply a myth recalled through a clumsy silhouette embroidered upon the state flag. What few puma and condor remain share the desolation of the Ventana wilderness and Sierra Madre, a land so precipitous and arid that man does not want it.

And those who are sensitive won't want to examine a detailed map of California's rivers too closely. For the Cascades and Sierras, feeding rivulet into creek into river—pure water from the Trinity Alps, Yosemite and Sequoia—are cut off, dammed, shunted and changed; diverted into reservoirs and canals, through power plants, into pipelines, then ultimately leached through chemical farmland to seep tepidly into the Delta or be rudely flushed down a toilet in Azusa.

Yet salmon, manifesting one of nature's more obvious wonders, still enter this vestigial river system. These, however, are not the brutes of once wild rivers but a resource that man beckons through a series of hatcheries. They are a domestic product, to stretch a term, based upon immutable instinct.

But there is one river left. Its tributaries gather freely and often fiercely beneath chiseled granite in the Siskiyou Mountains. Its water flows clear as air to later fold currentless into black-green pools that mirror looming redwoods and soaring osprey. Here in the Smith, the implacable king salmon come as they have throughout the millennium to reaffirm the unity of our sphere, to complete the complement of land mass to sea and season to season.

Several decades ago the lower reaches of the Eel River attracted fly-fishermen eager to catch steelhead. Sometimes large salmon were hooked by accident and accepted procedure was to break the line, thus terminating what was considered to be so one-sided a contest on behalf of the fish that these anglers wanted no part of it. It was never really made clear why the certainty of killing a five-pound steelhead was preferred to the challenge of trying to coerce a fifty-pound salmon.

"Not a fly-rod fish!" was all I was told.

Until very recently this antipathy kept the king salmon outside the realm of the fly-caster. Now the Smith River has become the specific in a sport that's captured the imagination of coastal anglers. Each fall, fishermen from all parts of the country gather in the northwest corner of California to intercept the cycle and possibly become part of a moment beyond mystery, reason or purpose.

I'd forgotten about the old prejudice until one day not long ago when a fisherman came down to a pool on the Smith where I was casting. He was an older man who had for years haunted the legendary Rogue. As he tied on a big fly and waded in, I noticed his fine old split-cane rod and classic English reel and thought to myself that it was an ill-advised, if explicable, choice of tackle.

Fishing had been very slow so I was surprised to see his rod immediately double against a salmon. He skillfully controlled his line, putting it tight to the reel and backed out of the water. I reeled in to be out of the way and watch.

"It's just like I thought," he remarked to me impatiently.

"Might as well hook an old boot."

An hour later the fish, which seemed to be about thirty pounds, still sawed easily in the current totally unaware of its predicament.

"How long does it take to get them in?" the man finally asked.

"Who knows?" I answered. "Yours doesn't even know it's hooked yet."

With a sigh the fisherman sidled downstream and pulled somewhat harder. In retaliation the salmon turned defiantly and began taking line in long, deliberate spasms. I knew precisely what was about to happen so I urged the man to start running or he'd be cleaned out. But he was frozen in his tracks, barely keeping a grip on the rod, which bent and recovered deeply. The reel vibrated ominously. Several nasty staccato cracks across his knuckles turned the angler's expression to one of abject horror and the slender rod strained impossibly toward the horizontal. Then, because of a compacted tangle deep in the backing, the rod splintered above the grip, the line broke at the reel and the "old boot" was free in a rocky throat far downstream.

Nearly in tears, the man raged, "I'll never fish for these damn things again!"

Naturally, fly-fishing for salmon on the Smith has acquired the dimensions of a scene, if only in a small way, compared with the much larger banality currently permeating the Gentle Sport. Around Crescent City you see a lot of arm patches and hats bristling with flies, whereas, nationally a player is likely to be identified with a fly or knot bearing his name, or more often, by the record book which lists an almost unending number of outrageously qualified accomplishments.

Angler: Flakey Foont. Species: Iowa darter. Bait or lure: Foont's Folly. Line: Size A Nymo thread. Remarks: Mr. Foont's fish (Etheostominae) though only six months old and weighing approximately one ounce, is a world record for a man fishing at three o'clock in the afternoon, using at Foont's Folly on sewing-thread tippet and wearing Ben Davis overalls while fly-casting in an abandoned irrigation ditch on the outskirts of Des Moines.

In the Smith the pound-test nonsense is minimized because, to put it directly, if you use a light leader you won't land any salmon.

Still there are an assortment of practitioners who take themselves and fishing quite seriously. There are also some serious fishermen. The former invite plenty of kidding but even in the case of the latter, the vagaries of the sport occasionally demand acknowledgment of a wide range of patent absurdities.

I arrived early one morning at a pool in which salmon were heavily concentrated. As might be expected, a large number of anglers crowded in to try their luck. At the top end, eight or ten fly-casters were working the swift flow, while below them about three dozen shore casters flung a variety of terminal tackle into the deep water. An access road allowed fishermen to drive onto the beach so that the gravel bar tended to resemble a used-car lot.

Several fish were hooked early on. The man next to me, by his own admission had never caught a salmon, but before long he set the hook into one which moved steadily away.

"Fish on here!" he cried in a voice one would normally only associate with a call for the police.

"It's in the dorsal," one of the other fly-fishermen offered.
"What?"

"He means you have him in the back," I said. "It's against
the law to keep a snagged fish, so you'll save yourself a lot of
trouble if you just break the line right now."

The man looked as though it had been suggested he slash
his wrists. "It's taken me a week to get hold of one of these
things," he stated, "and I'm not breaking any line until I see
with my own eyes where it's hooked."

At that moment the salmon left the water in a soaring end
over end leap, picking up a couple of other lines in the process. It landed with a thunderous explosion then raced off
downstream with the fisherman running along after it. The
lineup of hapless dunkers backed off in succession like a row
of card soldiers as the angler stumbled past screaming, "Fish
on! Fish on!"

"You don't suppose they're going to launch that thing in
here do you?" someone said nearby, and I turned my attention to the beach where an old pickup truck was straining to
tow a huge boat and trailer toward the water. "Look at the
size of that motor!"

In an hour the two men had managed to manhandle the
sixteen-foot boat into the river. Now they were loading it with
cushions, ice chest, tackle boxes, long-handled net and half a
dozen rods.

"They're shoving off," I commented.

The current was rather stiff and the craft began drifting
circularly into the midst of the pool where everyone was
fishing. One of the men tried the oars but could only manage
to flail the air so the other leaned over the engine and began
pulling on the starter cord.

"Not that!" I heard someone shout just as the huge jet engine caught. Its roar filled the peaceful canyon as the boat began charging around in a series of uncontrolled doughnuts. Waders backed off and men who had been standing to fly-cast in their little seven- and eight-foot prams sat down and gripped their gunwales as concentric wakes threatened to overturn them. The dark green water became light with foam and bubbles and the man next to me screamed, "Shut it off!" but I only know this because I read his lips.

The driver finally straightened the motor so the boat surged down the length of the pool sending the bank fishermen there scurrying for their rods to reel their lines in out of the way. Soon the craft was far below, near the man who was still fooling with the snagged fish. We could see him waving his arms in distress. Then I guess the men looked back and realized they had gotten out of the good fishing spot because they turned around and headed back.

After slicing through the pool once more, the man in the bow reached down and came up with an enormous navy anchor, which he dumped over the side when the other man cut the engine directly in front of the row of fly-casters. There was silence except for the slap of diminishing wavelets against the bank and the low murmur of obscenities.

One of the fly-casters addressed the pair somehow casually, yet in the sternest of tones. "Let me ask you gentlemen something," he began. "If you had a small bowl full of goldfish and you stuck a large electric mixer into it and ran it at top speed for ten minutes, then shut it off and dropped some goldfish food into the bowl, do you think they'd eat it?"

In spite of the wave of laughter, the men looked uncomprehendingly until someone else demanded point-blank, "Pull that anchor and get back here with the rest of us so we can all fish."

"Oh sure," they agreed. "Sorry, we're real new at this."

"Wait! No . . ."

Too late. The man in the back started the engine and the boat lunged forward, then banked around and they shut it down twenty feet back from where they had been and again heaved out the anchor. Despair.

More people were constantly arriving. It was now almost impossible to make more than two or three casts without picking up a line from across the river. There were constant cries of "Fish on!" followed closely by moans as rods doubled against one another. Salmon were almost forgotten as you tried to get a cast through without someone hooking your line.

A kid in a blue sweater came down with a couple of friends and began fishing opposite me. For a while I managed to avoid him by timing my casts with his. Finally he fooled me though and lobbed a bait over my line.

"The kid in blue is going to get a hit," I said.

I felt his sinker drag over my line and I let it swing until I felt we were firmly entangled, then I tightened up. He struck. But he was cautious, glancing over to see if anyone else was pulling but I kept my rod down pretending to be fishing.

Then he cut loose. "Got one!" he screamed. "Fish on! Ralph, Billy, get the net!" Gradually our lines rose and sprang above the surface swinging slowly back and forth.

"I'm sorry, I think I've hooked your line," I called.

Someone was always hooked on the bottom and it was fun to watch the different ways people had of breaking their lines to get free. For example, you had "the man hoeing weeds," or the "hula dancer." Anyway, snagging bottom had become known as a *five*, a term that baffled the uninitiated. Earlier in the year we fished a pool that was so full of obstructions that lure and bait casters couldn't fish it. We arrived at the expression *five* because more often than not they would hook bottom on five casts out of five, in which case it was a *perfect five*. If the method of breaking the line were amusing or interesting enough, this was known as a *classic five*. There is just something basically funny about a grown man pulling on a fish line stuck to the bottom.

The fly-fishermen hooked bottom a lot too so there was always a big demand for more flies. I noticed a man next to me looking into the water.

"There's a fly down there," he said. "It's a beauty too."

For the next fifteen minutes he grappled with his rod tip, trying to get it.

"Got it!" he announced. "Look, it's even got a leader on it. Wait a minute. Oh no . . ." The leader was in turn attached to his own line.

Some of the fly-fishermen were in boats and others were wading, though all were in line, fishing the same water. There were so many people milling around on the beach you had to watch your backcast pretty closely because it would extend into a zone where non-fishermen were forever wandering.

One angler, intent upon his fishing, was preparing to lean into a cast when a loud yell went up from the beach. He had forgotten to look and it seemed he'd buried his salmon fly in a lady's fundament. Without a moment's hesitation she ran to her car, jumped in, slammed the door and drove off. As the sedan lurched away the angler's reel screamed until the line finally broke.

Toward dark I thought I had a strike but so many different people set the hook it was hard to tell. Three rods were half-circled on the other side. I gave slack and watched, concluding we all had one fish or perhaps more simple, one another.

It did seem, however, that there was a fish in on it somewhere.

Meanwhile a fish was hooked upstream and another below. Naturally, the one downstream headed up and vice versa. In the process a lot of bank fishermen, who had strolled away from their rods, found their lines being dragged into the mess. There were shouts of, "Let loose! Let loose!" I stood idly by, holding my fly rod at my side like a man with a newspaper waiting for a bus. Across the river I could see the three conferring over their lines.

The man below cursed loudly when he lost his fish in the shuffle. I looked up and the fly-fisherman who'd had the other fish was busily tying on a new fly. My line still stretched over the river where the three were now backing away from one another, moving their arms in corkscrew motions. Finally my line went directly to one individual's hands then slanted down into the water.

"Hey mister," he called. "I think maybe you got a fish on there."

I reeled in the loose line to find he was right. Not only was there a fish but I could feel by the shaking of its head that it was fair-hooked. I routinely began to play it the way the man with the newspaper would have boarded his bus. As I did so a contingent of the Now Generation grouped themselves behind me. Even in the chill of evening they were barefoot and wore an assortment of loose vests, floppy hats and heavy necklaces. One carried a short fishing rod with a pushbutton reel. I remembered seeing him earlier, flipping a spoon carelessly into the water the way another might discard a candy wrapper.

"Hey man," one inquired slackly. "You got one?"

"Yes."

"Far out. We'd dig seeing one up close."

Before long the salmon was veering near the beach having spent most of its energy earlier fighting four people. It was a brilliant female close to forty pounds.

"Want us to grab that mother for ya?"

"No, no," I insisted. "I can manage."

In a moment I had forced the salmon against the beach.

"Outta sight, man! That'd feed the whole commune."

I looked at the fish in the fading light and considered the appetites of the communal dwellers. The salmon's eye focused downward toward the tiny fly lodged in the corner of its mouth and momentarily I pictured it cruising beneath the polar ice cap foraging for shrimp. I wondered at the events that led it back to this river to ultimately seize the treacherous hook which brought it to lie on this gravel bar and be ogled and discussed by a lunatic from the Rocky Mountains and a group of dropouts from San Francisco.

The fly came free with relative ease and I held the fish upright in the water for a few moments until it undulated away into the dark.

The kid with the pushbutton reel spoke. "Man, if I get me one of those I ain't gonna throw it away."

"You probably won't have to worry," I said.

Chapter Six

TIME AND TIDE

Salmon and steelhead forage widely on the open ocean in a dining room bound only by the continents, and this vastness implies perfectly the breadth of spirit these noble fish embody. To understand the salmon, it has been said, would be to crack the universe.

Unerringly, salmon come around their wheel to spawn and

die at the place where they were born. So do steelhead, the great trout of the sea, though for them death is not always imminent. And while salmon are frequently taken inland in addition to providing the bulk of both the commercial and sport catch off the West Coast of North America, steelhead are rarely caught at sea.

Immmediately before becoming riverbound both fish can be taken at their prime. Consider the cycle: one to five years of intense feeding solely to gain strength to survive the spawning journey. Clearly these fish are at their finest just prior to entering fresh water before using stored energy as they must when feeding ceases.

There are distinct stages in the lives of anadromous fish: river, transition, ocean, transition, river. The transitional periods are by far the shortest and it is the second of these that interests the angler.

As the migrants near shore their habitat gains a definition it didn't have at sea. In open water, trolling is the only practical way of fishing for salmon. But as the procreative urge draws the fish near his river or creek, the wader and rowboat fishermen have their day. Now, steelhead, too, become game for the angler and it is the only time in their salt-water life when this is so.

In a defined area fishing is more absorbing. For example, in off-shore waters a thirty-pound salmon will make runs and dart about, perhaps even jump, but without any bottom or shore to relate himself to, he can usually be led close enough to be netted rather quickly. Assuming leader strength to be similar, that same thirty-pounder will give twice the battle in a tidal estuary because it is in the fish's nature to seek cover when it is available. You can be sure that if there is a brush pile nearby—as there so often is in a tidal reach—the salmon will try and get into it. Too, the fish will frantically avoid being led into shallow water.

Perhaps both species are slightly uneasy upon first entering confined water after years of living in an unlimited expanse. Somewhat cautious already then, when hooked it could be they are prepared to wage a more desperate battle. The fish is fighting for his life and never before has he had more reason to live.

I've fished the estuary of Paper Mill Creek and Tomales Bay into which it flows for almost a quarter of a century. During the first of those I was a spinning enthusiast but soon learned the greater joy of fly-fishing. More than that, I came to know above all it was the tide that spelled the difference between success and failure.

One year at Christmas there had been no rain for nearly three weeks. This left Paper Mill Creek itself extremely low and clear. No fish could move out of the estuary into it. It was time for the main run of steelhead to appear but I tried the usual holding places and neither caught nor saw any. It was obvious they hadn't gone through because you could see into all the holes upstream (where fishing is illegal) and there were only a few spent silvers.

The remaining possibility was that they were still in Tomales Bay. The odds against successfully searching such large water, especially with a fly rod, seemed so overwhelmingly high I put off trying and instead went duck hunting the next day. It was a fortuitous move for quite by accident I found the fish.

There was a two-foot minus low tide in midafternoon that completely dried out the mud flats near Inverness. I'd thought to stalk some pintails which were sitting on a mud spit when suddenly I saw a fish's wake in several inches of water. Moments later there was another that surged erratically over the flat. Thinking they were striped bass I got the binoculars and saw clearly that instead they were steelhead. The wakes were disappearing into a small basin I knew was about three feet deep. Of course! On the big minus tide, the basin was one of the few places in the upper bay with any water in it.

Next day I arrived with a fly rod about noon. The tide was still much too high but it was rushing out rapidly. Since I knew precisely where the basin was even on the flood, having fished it many times for stripers, I waded out in a burst of early enthusiasm and made a few casts preferring that to just sitting and waiting for the tide to drop. Right away, in a stroke of luck unequaled before or since, I had a fish on. Twenty minutes later a fine twelve-pound female steelhead lay exhausted at my feet.

For an hour after that too easy triumph, I cast diligently but caught nothing so I sat down to wait it out. Two hours later the flats in front of me had only three or four inches of water over them and that was when the first wake appeared. But I didn't catch a fish until after seeing half a dozen more. With the tide dropping, the current became confined to the tiny channel and ran stiffly through the basin. Positioned slightly upstream, I began to cast, quartering down with a light number-six line which sank very slowly. On the third or fourth swing a fish took and tail-walked twenty yards to the far edge of the basin then ran back, half out of water. In a few minutes it had been caught and released. Fishing was extraordinary until dark. The fishing diary I used to keep reads, ". . . Dec. 28 . . . 15 steelhead hooked . . . 11 landed . . . 6 to 12 lbs."

Conditions lasted five more days. At the end of that time the minus tides were not severe enough to force the fish into the pocket and the lows were too late at night to be of any use. Besides, the fish moved to a different spot but that's another story. I was glad no one ever spotted me because a single unscrupulous fisherman could have literally wiped out the run. Altogether the log book shows fifty-seven fish on the beach all released but one—the first I caught that day on the high tide. Three I caught twice and two were foul-hooked due to the confined area. The single critical factor contributing to this good fishing, aside from the fact that the fish were there, was the tide. The spot was no good on anything less than a 1.5 minus because it took that little water to force the steelhead to bunch up in the basin.

A few miles north of San Francisco Muir Creek flows out of the famed Redwood National Park to join the Pacific. It is a tiny stream and like so many others, fish can enter it only after a substantial rain. In October silvers gather off its mouth and must occasionally wait until late December to spawn. Often they are joined in the surf by steelhead. Many years ago there was a dry winter and while both fish waited along the beach they could be seen leaping in the surf. I caught a number of them that fall in what was for me an unprecedented experience. Early on the fish were bright but by December most were dark and had formed the kype or hooked jaw associated with mature spawning fish. Salmon turn dark in relation to their state of maturity rather than because they've entered fresh water. Some of these appeared to be trying to spawn right on the beach, nosed against a spot where perhaps a trace of fresh water seeped through the sand.

In all tidewater fishing it is impossible to emphasize too strongly how critical the action of the tide is. As a rule the fresher the fish the better they seem to bite on the high water, particularly the top of the ebb. The larger runouts seem to activate fish also at least in sloughs and estuaries where there is a river-like flow.

An interesting point is that fresh silvers generally swim relatively near the surface. These are the ones that bite best on the high water. If these same fish are forced to lay for some time in tidewater before getting upstream, they seem to settle deeper as they would in a river pool and the older they get the farther down on the tide they bite.

Frank Allen took one such silver about fifteen years ago in Paper Mill's estuary. That fish weighed close to twenty-two pounds and at the time was clearly a world fly-casting record. Frank had wanted to release the fish because it was dark but the late Joe Paul persuaded him to keep it saying it was surely a record. It was, but Frank was happy just to have caught it and never bothered to try for official recognition.

This pattern of new fish biting on the high water and older fish on the low is observable in many streams. On the Chetco River in Oregon old fish are most apt to be caught in the Morrison or Tide Rock Holes at the end of the outgoing tide. The fresh fish from Morrison on down to Snug Harbor seem to bite best on the high rise and high ebb.

During fall in California—Oregon, too, for that matter—all the short coastal streams are at their lowest. In creeks like Paper Mill little fresh water is present in the lagoons. The same could be said of rivers such as the Gualala, Garcia, Navarro and lower Eel below the Snag Hole. On several occasions I've caught silvers in the lagoon at Navarro on the high incoming tide when waves from the nearby ocean were rolling far up the river.

Once I had an excellent time just inside the bar of Redwood Creek at Orick. A run of small king salmon called chubs had just entered the lagoon. When I saw them rolling I launched an eight-foot boat and, with only the gulls and crashing sea for company, caught a number of them.

Onc fall I caught silvers in Tomales Bay fly-casting from my pram. Actually I was out for stripers but when the salmon kept jumping near the boat I tied on a comet and caught three in about two hours.

There has always been a "run" of salmon and steelhead in Bodega Bay. Ostensibly, the reason for it is that at one time nearby Salmon Creek emptied into Bodega at its north end. Even now some fresh water seeps in there. Some claim it is Salmon Creek water though the creek itself enters the sea a mile or so to the north. When its sandbar is closed, some fish find their way into Bodega, perhaps sensing the source of this seepage. Some exciting mornings have passed here when the fish were jumping within casting range. A floating line and smallish shrimp fly worked for me, especially on the high tide.

In Pescadero Creek, south of San Francisco, local anglers fish the high incoming tide when that stream is muddy from winter rains. For a few hours each day the rising water and heavy surge push the dirty water some distance back up the slough and casters fish the clear ocean water hoping to take bright steelhead fresh in from the sea.

The best day of steelhead fishing I ever had was in salt water at the junction of Paper Mill's estuary and Tomales Bay. It was near the end of February, so of course these were downstreamers—fish already spawned and on their way back to sea—but they proved to be vigorous quarry nevertheless.

I arrived about nine on a quiet overcast morning. The tide was halfway out and the water was clear. I fished carefully through the pool for an hour without luck. Somewhat discouraged I sat down to enjoy being alone on the beautiful moor. The tide had fallen a foot or so since I'd arrived and the current had slowed. As I sat thinking of other things, a fish rolled in the center of the hole. I got up and made a hurried cast. Five strips into the retrieve the fish took, then jumped end for end several times before I could beach it, remove my fly and turn it loose. The steelhead would have weighed about six pounds and was in healthy condition. The bottom of its tail was just slightly abrased as in all spent steelhead and it still retained its silver color.

Soon I had another strike and again landed a six-pounder identical in appearance to the first. After releasing it I caught another. And another. At the peak of the bite, hits were coming regularly on every cast. Gradually the fish moved down toward the lower end of the pool so it took longer and longer casts to reach them. Finally, about three o'clock they were gone.

The tide turned and started to rise, but I couldn't get another strike. It was as though there'd never been any fish. Strangely, all during the time I was catching them there was never any surface indication that steelhead were present. The first fish that rolled was the only one all day.

To quote the log again, ". . . Feb. 27 . . . 32 takes . . . 23 fish landed . . . all 6 lbs." This last seems nothing short of remarkable for each fish was nearly identical to the next and even more, fought similarly. It was quite like catching the same fish again and again as in a film being reshown. And not once did the leader break. The same little black and orange fly stayed tied to the tippet throughout.

Before leaving I notched the thin trunk of one of the moor's few bushes twenty-three times and imbedded the fly below that. Ten years later the notches were no longer visible and the fly had rotted away leaving a bare, rusted hook protruding enigmatically from the bush's stem. Today, no doubt, all that's left is the memory.

Chapter Seven

SHAD FISHING REVISITED

It is a typically cold, foggy June morning as I and two companions leave San Francisco on the drive to Marysville and Yuba City where we will spend the day shad fishing. We may perhaps fish the Feather River but ostensibly our goal is the smaller, clearer Yuba.

These streams wind through California's Central Valley, which reaches north and south from its broad delta like a soulful inlay between the austere Sierra Nevada Mountains and the outrageous, often porcine hordes of people on the coast. Here, one is sometimes reminded of the Deep South.

We leave the fog behind near Vallejo and at Vacaville the valley opens up and we see an improbably red, oblong sun clear the horizon like a drop of mercury, a brief overture to its searing trajectory over corn and wheat and rice.

As usual it will be hot. A temperature of above a hundred would not be unusual. At 6:30 A.M. the waitress in the restaurant pulls the shades while the air conditioner annoyingly ruffles the surface of our coffee.

Through a window at the end of the cafe I notice one of the old "Giant Orange" stands, now abandoned and overgrown. Before Highway 40 became Interstate 80 these preposterous hot dog and soft drink emporiums stood beside the roadway at intervals between Sacramento and San Francisco, inviting summer travelers with their citric silhouettes. The invitation may have been aimed more at the customer's curiosity—or sense of humor—than his culinary discretion, but after our waitress admonishes us about "substitutions" I reflect they had a quality perhaps more direct, innocent and even appealing than does the tiresome chain of twenty-four-hour restaurants which has replaced them.

Back in the car I learn my friends have never been shad fishing and in the midst of our conversation about it I miss our turnoff, which was Route 113, and am on the Yolo Causeway before I realize it. We must go all the way to Sacramento where we can then take Route 99. It is a dark moment for me as a guide and I momentarily consider the notion of telling my friends I thought we should have a look at the American River first, before going all the way to the Yuba.

In an hour we are in Marysville where I manage to remember the railroad tracks, the levee and then the road that crosses the river and skirts the golf course. It is then straight to Hammonton where there is a place to fish.

But today the gate at Hammonton is locked. It has never been locked before and I wonder if there is a way to get permission, so we drive around to the office of the Yuba Consolidated Gold Company. A secretary there is very polite but informs me that the tab will be three dollars a head. Nine dollars that would be just to see the river and how do we even know there will be any shad there? We decide to keep our nine dollars and start back toward town.

Many little roads lead away from the one we are on and run in the direction of the river which cannot be far away because we see the cottonwoods and willows which border it. We try some of these roads but there is always a NO TRESPASSING sign just at the point beyond which we would hopefully go fishing.

I rue the locked gate and remember the sign posted during the previous season. It was a warning to fishermen that if they did not stop abusing the land in the form of littering, they—Yuba Consolidated—would be forced to fence them out, i.e. "no fishing."

How the fishermen could further ruin the already murdered, violated and dismembered property makes an interesting question, because the whole area on both sides of the river from Marysville upstream to the dam has literally been turned upside down, leaving perhaps seventy-five square miles of cobblestone tailings wherein a scattering of cottonwood, elderbery, oak, willow and sycamore grasp a precarious footing around the deep holes left by the dredgers.

It is not land, there really is no land left, just property. Yet the semblance of an erstwhile glorious river still continues to hold enough basic wildness to resist so well man's pollution of streams and lakes, in this case pollution for gold.

Some of these dredgers still sit in the middle of their lakes trying to rust while men take care of them year round. Gravel is taken from the bottom at one end of the dredger, then spewed in endlessly belching arcs at the other, building mound upon mound of sterile rock. In the spring, swallows come to nest amid the complexities of the equipment and swoop among the moonscape tailings which are being remade.

The vast machines operate around the clock and at night are beautifully and mysteriously lit, and their voices become more patent so that one is moved to dwell upon them. The sound is an amalgamation of scrapes, clanks and squeaks into a distant wail that easily embarrasses the best efforts of John Cage. If you are camping nearby, you will listen to this protest, this far-out music, because the mosquitoes will awaken you to insist you listen.

In Marysville I wonder if we should look at the Feather near Shanghai Bend which is only a few miles below town. Over the years it has been a consistently good place to catch shad, so we cross over into Yuba City and drive down behind the levee.

Again we find a road that is cabled off but I notice a track through the orchard and construe the fresh tire marks as license to trespass.

We arrive at the base of the levee and after climbing it are on a bluff overlooking the river. It is high and roily. Discouraged, I think of the backwater just upstream where a friend once caught any number of large bullfrogs by dangling his shad fly in front of them. It is a certainty that we will not be catching any shad at Shanghai Bend today.

But I recall one torrid afternoon some years earlier when Phil Wood and I sat on this same bluff looking down on a low clear river and we were worn out from catching considerably more shad than we really wanted to, at least by the method it took to catch them which involved fast-sinking fly lines and weighted flies. Across from us was a vast beach that curved clear out of sight. Along its perimeter we noted with interest that many hundreds of shad were working along the surface.

During the past decade it has become popular to set a numerical criterion for success at a hundred fish a day. The thing is, it's entirely possible to drag a hundred or more of these oversize herring ashore, providing you have no objections to behaving like a figure in the Musée Méchanique. Somehow though, the idea of simply catching lots of fish doesn't go very far.

A peculiarity of the sport is that shad are all about the same size, which is to say from two to five pounds. The average is about three and the odd individual could go seven or eight. You don't fish with the idea that you could get a really big one as you might with black bass or salmon.

Too, shad seem to either strike or not according to their mood and it's never really a matter of using the right fly, as is often the instance in fishing for selective trout. The only important consideration insofar as the fly is concerned is its size. When the water is low and clear, shad definitely prefer smaller, less garish flies.

The epitome of shad fishing is to catch them on light, refined tackle near the surface, or right on top with a dry fly. I'm told that the smaller hickory shad take free-floating drys in some of the lesser streams along the East Coast. In the

West I've always had to drag the fly slightly in order to get strikes and even then conditions had to be perfect. Anyway, it would seem the astute angler would seek quality and consider quantity, if it should materialize, a bonus.

So, wanting the best the sport could offer, Phil and I triangulated the location of the beach where all the shad were swimming, and went back to the car. After driving to Yuba City, then across the bridge into Marysville, we found a road that paralleled the river. On the way we looked for church steeples, silos, anything that might bear upon the location of the beach.

At a point we thought seemed right, the road led over a levee so we took it and drove between wide fields toward a small cluster of buildings, pulling up to the small ranch house. Our dust filtered past to turn the afternoon sun red-ochre.

The door to the house stood open and through it we could see what was evidently a Saturday-night party getting underway. Phil knocked and an immense black man holding a can of beer appeared. From behind him loud jazz rocked forth and there was laughing.

"Yes?"

"We," Phil began, with a nod at me, "have driven here from San Francisco to go shad fishing and saw your beautiful beach from across the river and wondered if we could get permission to go through your property to get to it."

The large man looked down at us for some moments before answering. "Wel-l-l . . ." he said. "Since you *asked* me!" Then there was a long pause. "Now since you *asked* me!" A long pause again during which several other people at the party crowded curiously at the door. "Since you have *asked* me, it'll be all right. Drive on out past that chicken coop, then keep to the right of the barn. In fact, the whole way you want to keep to the right. After a bit you'll pass a shed and tractor, then when you hit the fresh-plowed field you're about there."

Thanking him, we started off, bearing right until we were deep into heavy underbrush that obscured what we had been using as a road. Rocks slammed mercilessly into the oil pan until we came to the freshly plowed field which covered rocks and road under six inches of silt.

During the last of it we coursed our way painfully beside a very unstable-looking arroyo which fell away on the passenger's side for thirty feet or more. Foreseeing the possibility of an unplanned descent, Phil got out and walked beside the car —I was driving—presumably so he could direct me if such a need arose.

We reached a point where it was impossible to continue so we left the car, taking our tackle, and began to walk. It was a very long quarter mile through loose sand which seemed to drag us back, but we knew it would be well worth the trouble for the spectacular surface fishing that awaited.

Finally we stepped onto the perfect beach and stood for some moments watching the river. It was almost too much to accept: the shad were all on the other side of the river right where we had been. Nonetheless, we maintained our enthusiasm saying that surely they would again move over into the shallow water. But we cast until dark and caught absolutely nothing.

Slogging back to the car in the night, surrounded by a swarm of mosquitoes, tripping in the deep loam, we both started to giggle hysterically. We were sitting down and through his choking laughter, Phil imitated the man back at the ranch. "Wel-l-l . . . since you *asked* me!"

So Shanghai Bend is out. It is now almost noon and my companions are beginning to call into question my ability to show them a shad. I reason that with the river so high it is logical to assume, imperative perhaps, that whatever fish are in the river have migrated as far up as they can go which means the Oroville dam.

I hold out vague hope for Gridley where I have often had good fishing but there is only one man there and he is fishing for catfish. He assures us the only place they are catching any shad is at the dam. I haven't fished the Feather since the dam was completed so we get directions in Gridley and start off.

Actually, we find out the shad cannot get anywhere near the dam itself, nor can we. There is a maze of spillways, reservoirs, diversions and weirs extending some miles below the actual dam, while the natural riverbed wanders off like a kind of sorry appendix.

After passing through a lot of dry countryside made institutional by miles of cyclone fence, we arrive at a spillway below something called the Thermolito Afterbay. There, large schools of shad are gulping air.

One of my friends is an accomplished fly-caster. The other, I realize, will have difficulty getting much more than about thirty feet, so we walk to the end of the spillway where the water is very deep and I sternly advise him to cast into the near current where fish can be seen splashing and let his fly swing around below him.

Immediately he begins catching shad. In fact, we all start catching them but not nearly so many as he. However, we are having a lot of fun and catch and release quite a few.

Shortly, a man comes walking down the gravel incline and stops nearby. "You boys better not let the warden catch you here."

"Oh?"

"He got some guys yesterday. Too close to the spillway."

We reel in, thank him, look around for the signs that seem to be missing, then drive some distance downstream where we pull in among the willows. It is not a particularly good place to fish, certainly not as good as the spot at the dam, but we wade into the water and start fishing anyway.

There are a number of spin fishermen perched along the bank who are taking a few fish. A man in a cowboy hat is anchored out in the river and he seems to have a shad on every cast. Upstream from us a family has fanned out into a shallow riffle and are casting into the current. Among them is a toothsome young lady who draws our attention because of her bikini, which is so small that we are sure it will soon fail its task.

Shad seem plentiful as we are into them right away, though my friend whose casting ability is limited is again catching the most. Before long, the girl wades down to us carrying a metal stringer and asks if her father can have our shad since we don't want them because he has a smokehouse. We agree to keep some and she wonders aloud why we want to fish if we are going to throw them all back. I explain for the thrill in the catch.

A rather banal conversation ensues wherein the girl, having taken a fancy to, God Knows Why, the one among us inept at his sport, goes into some detail describing her disinterest in fishing, shad fishing in particular. She wants to be back home in Daly City, not stuck out here in the boondocks. She wants to have a fun summer before she starts her job with the phone company in the fall. In short, she is bored stiff.

My friend lets her bring in the shad he is hooking with disgusting regularity until she is squealing with delight. Her father's stringer is growing heavy with fish. Meanwhile, the father himself remains stubbornly in the shallows, pant legs rolled up, catching nothing.

My other companion and I continue to fish as if it mattered while our third and the girl gradually abandon angling in favor of splashing each other and finally, just plain swimming.

It is late in the afternoon when it is time for us to leave. The girl asks where we are going to camp, suggesting we could get together later that evening. When we tell her we are going back to San Francisco she appears desperate, and dejectedly takes her dad's stringer full of shad and rejoins her family.

During the ride home I am apologetic about the generally poor quality of the fishing.

"Oh, I don't know," my neophyte friend insists. "It seemed pretty good to me."

Chapter Eight

DESERT TROUT

From San Francisco east into the Sierra, the foothills build
gradually so that you have a very complete sense of entering
the mountains. Then the summit breaks away toward Donner
Lake and the Truckee River watershed. Sheer rock walls slice
down to the riverbed, so it is surprising when the canyon
flares abruptly, opening to meadows and plain. Out there sits
the town of Reno.

My mother, who spends a certain amount of her time at the gaming tables, had called from one of the clubs. "Hello, dear. They tell me the loud-mouth trout fishing is good right now."

"What?"

"You know, in Pyramid Lake. Didn't you say you wanted me to call if the loud-mouth fishing was good?"

"You mean cutthroat trout."

"Yes, that's what I said. It's good right now."

So I was heading out into the Nevada desert. It had been an unusually mild winter. The snow pack was light, about what you would expect in May, yet it was February. After stopping in Reno for a license and the permit needed to fish on Indian land, I drove into the peopleless sink country, blasting along through an intimidating expanse of brush and distant mesas. From a rise in the Paiute Reservation I had my first view of the lake. In the bright sunlight it appeared small, deceptively so, stretching to the north and south like a swath of cobalt paint. Later, arriving at some buildings and trailers known as Sutcliffe, I found a dock and launching ramp. A boat had just come in, and a man got out carrying a fish that easily weighed ten pounds. It was the largest cutthroat I had ever seen.

After minutes of watching the lake I began to understand its vastness as several boats trolled on its perfect surface, so far away they were mere specks. "Is it deep?" I asked an Indian. "Yes," he said. "When they drown we never find them."

I drove south along the shore and pulled off the road near a rocky point. I got into a pair of waders and strung up a rod. Fishermen in the area believe a woolly worm is the best fly and that it should be fished deep and slow. What these flies represent, if anything, is a mystery. However, the lake is rich in food—there is an abundance of snails and plankton—and when the trout move into shallow water near the shore these non-descript patterns account for most of the catch.

When the sun began to drop out of sight a Jeep lurched to a stop nearby and a man with a spinning rod got out, walked immediately to the water's edge and began to cast. We were perhaps a hundred feet apart when there was a tremendous splash between us. The man called out something I could not quite hear and seemed to indicate I should cast to the fish. I did, but nothing happened. When it became too dark to fish we talked for a moment near his car. "When they surface like that one did," he told me, "cast right away and you stand a good chance. But the weather's just too nice for good fishing. The nastier it is the better the fish bite. Thought I might have a chance of hitting one right at dark, though. By the way, you want to be careful in those waders. Bottom's tricky. They lost a guy last week and haven't found him."

Pyramid Lake is part of what's left of an inland sea originally called Lake Lahontan—Walker Lake is also a remnant of the once-huge body of water—and the Lahontan trout, a species of cutthroat, is seldom found outside this area. Both lakes are highly alkaline due to intense evaporation, and the Nevada Fish and Game Department feels that Walker may have no more than twenty years left as a fresh-water fishery.

On the other hand, Pyramid is large and deep with a freshwater inflow from the Truckee River. The lake began to get in trouble in the thirties as more and more of the Truckee water was diverted for irrigation purposes. This forced the magnificent Lahontan trout to the brink of extinction by 1940. The forty-one-pounder caught in 1925 by a Paiute remains the largest cutthroat trout ever taken anywhere in the world.

For years the Fish and Game Department has kept Pyramid alive by rigorously stocking a pure strain of the native trout as well as rainbow-cutthroat hybrids. And in October 1974 the Interior Department announced it would cancel the old Irrigation District contract, taking over control of the Truckee River water. Limiting the amount of water that can be diverted for irrigation can help the Lahontan trout. The flow over the Truckee delta will increase, and the fish will more easily reach the river to spawn naturally.

The following afternoon I headed for the south end of the lake near the river mouth. Here there was a beach that seemed a popular fishing spot. Several anglers were casting woolly-worm flies on spinning tackle with thin pencil sinkers attached. They had been at it all day and some had set up folding chairs by the water. As I watched, one man caught a hybrid of about four pounds. But I wanted to take a pure Lahontan trout. The beach seemed terribly tame so I drove north around the lake looking for a place that might offer solitude. I found a setting deeply arcane and wanted to cultivate this sense of mystery.

The air was cool, and a gusty, changeable wind ruffled the lake. I wondered if conditions were adverse enough to provide good fishing. I found a small feeder stream, or more accurately, a spring. The high bank was troublesome so I quartered the line as I worked along the shore. I cast, let the fly sink, then retrieved it in slow pulls. The lake dropped off sharply here, and when the line stopped I knew it was a fish.

It did not jump or dash wildly about, but chugged strongly, staying deep. I flushed with excitement when it veered off the bank, splashing water as it turned to run. I nervously led it against the gravel, and reaching down saw it had none of the characteristic marks of the rainbow. It was dark, almost green on the back, and had a few spots, mostly near the tail. Under its gills were two bright dashes of red-orange. At that moment one could sense the qualities of the desert and appreciate the fragile hold this diminishing body of water maintained on it. I imagined the trout would weigh a bit under five pounds. I removed the fly and placed the fish back in the water. It was gone in an instant, leaving only the wind and gathering dusk.

Reno blazed into the icy night as I entered my hotel through the casino. The din and the chrome were too much. I walked straight through and out the other side. Across the street I saw an inauspicious establishment whose sign proclaimed TOPLESS. I poked my head in—there were no slot machines and no customers. Three or four girls sat around laughing and talking.

A girl named Carol asked if I would buy her a drink. We played the jukebox and began talking. At one point she excused herself because it was her turn to dance, whipped off her halter, grinned through a number, came back and sat down.

"What brings you here if you don't like to gamble?" she asked.

"I'm fishing for trout in Pyramid Lake."

"Well, you be careful, honey," she said. "If you drown in there they'll never find you."

Chapter Nine

AN AUDIENCE WITH HIS MAJESTY

"There's one." Bill Schaadt's voice was excited yet firm. He was backing deliberately out of the water and from the tip of his arched fly rod, line angled far out into the deepest part of the pool where white specks of foam slid over dark water. Frank Bertaina, Jack Geib, Bob Nauheim, Ben Miller, Sid Green and I reeled in our lines as Bill's fish swung strongly downstream.

On the other side of California's Smith River, moss grew heavily on angular rocks lifting and pushing the strong current into an eddy. A damp thicket disappeared beneath the towering monarchs of Jedediah Smith Park. On the floor of the redwood forest, in eternal silence, mushrooms grew where the sun had not shown for a thousand years.

Otters lived along the riverbank here, capturing an occasional fish. Bear and deer found refuge in the tangled woods, while overhead the osprey and eagle soared. In the icy river lunging beneath the flow, was the king salmon.

"He's gone," lamented Bill as his line trailed loosely away downstream. "That's the twelfth one in a row I've lost. If the hook doesn't pull out the leader breaks, if the leader holds they go in the snags. They're tough, that's all."

As we all went back to fishing I could hear Nauheim mumbling something under his breath about the ultimate challenge. Bertaina shook his head and chuckled enigmatically. Beyond him, Geib, Miller and Green went methodically about their casting. Somewhat separated from the rest, Bill Schaadt focused his boundless energy on the water before him.

Hours passed to the roar of rapids upstream and the musical rush of water against the far bank except when a salmon rolled, shattering the pool's surface and a murmur arose from among the anglers.

Not long after Bill lost his fish in the rocks he hooked another which he landed. It was a splendid forty-pounder but it turned out to be the only fish caught that day. We stayed until dark then met later at Grant King's place.

"I think I'll take a boat and try down below tomorrow," said Frank Bertaina. "The fish are thinning out up here.

Should be new ones coming in all the time." The others agreed.

The following morning I went back to the same pool and caught nothing. At noon I gave up and went downstream. One hole in particular had loaded up overnight with new fish. Schaadt, Miller, Nauheim and Bertaina had all hooked fish.

When I reached the beach, Frank offered to row me over to a high bank where we could see the fish. After climbing out on a rocky point, I saw them. Not only did their blue-gray color indicate they were fresh, silver, new, but they were enormous. Any number were over forty or fifty pounds. Sometimes they hung together in the current but more often circled the hole in a restless manner.

"Wait until you see the big one." Frank smiled.

Through my Polaroid glasses I watched, enthralled. Then, from under the rock glided a fish of staggering proportions.

"There he is," Frank whispered. "Spotted him this morning. A real monster. He's at least eighty pounds."

Schaadt was in his boat, casting. I tried to imagine what it would be like if that fish decided it wanted a small orange fly. We could see Bill's line and fly as they sank toward the salmon. But they would have none of it, especially the big one as it glided back out of sight.

The next morning I awoke unsure of where to start the day. I knew Bill would stay below. Perhaps Bob and Frank would do the same, along with Ben. There were already too many lines in the water down there so I decided to try a spot upriver, hoping new fish had moved during the night. When I arrived, another fisherman was already in the water. It was Jack Geib.

"Where is everyone?" he asked.

"They found fish down below yesterday," I answered. "We might have this to ourselves today."

Shortly thereafter, Jack put the first salmon of the day on. By midafternoon he'd hooked two dozen more and I'd hooked fifteen. Among the ones Jack landed was a dark male close to fifty pounds which he released.

We were ecstatic even as we saw opposite us a figure working his way up to the river through the brush. The figure materialized into Frank Bertaina, who climbed out on a high rock where he could look into the pool.

"Wondered where you guys were," he said, putting on his Polaroids. "Hate to tell you this but there's nothing in there."

"You mean we've spent all this time fishing in a dry hole?" I called, pretending to be shocked.

"I can't see a single fish in the pool," Frank replied.

"How did you do downstream?" Jack asked.

"We blanked out. The fish moved."

"We hooked a couple here," Jack offered with an ill-concealed smile.

Smelling a rat, Frank climbed over above the riffle where we were casting and again put on his glasses.

"Watch, Jack," I said, "this'll be interesting."

As Frank peered into the water we could see him catch his breath. Without saying a word he tore off his glasses, stuffed them in his jacket and began clawing his way up the bank.

Jack and I were still laughing when Frank charged out of the bushes behind us and ran across the gravel bar to the river.

"OK," he said, "how many, really?"

"About forty," Jack answered through a broad grin.

After finishing out the day we walked wearily back to the cars, where Jack advised, "Get down here early tomorrow.

There's going to be plenty of competition."

That night I had salmon fever. I dreamed of great fish cruising smoothly about pristine pools in almost unearthly splendor. Among them was one indomitable giant who seemed to defy his own destiny, to be immune to the inevitable death he must surely face before the year was out.

The moon was still up, and ice covered the beach next morning as I arrived at the river. Bill and Jack were already in the water. Soon, Ben, Bob and Frank appeared. Young Buzz Bergman, Grant King, John Bach and several other anglers came later. No one wanted to miss this chance.

Several fish were hooked early on. After snagging bottom for what seemed like the hundredth time, I reached in my pocket to find myself out of leader material. In a hurry and not wanting to bother anyone I glanced at the beach and saw numerous tangles of discarded spinning line. Immediately I found some that looked undamaged and of at least twelve-pound test. Hastily, I tied it on, rushing back into the water.

Sometime later I brought the fly in to check it after snagging bottom again and saw a knot in the leader. I couldn't get it out so I decided to cinch it up, make a cast, reel in and borrow some decent material from Frank.

My half-hearted cast landed and started to swing. At that moment Frank struck a fish. Seconds later my line pulled up and I thought it was over his. I began to blurt a lame apology, then saw his rod was straight.

"Don't you have one?" I asked quickly.

"Foul-hooked. Broke him off."

I came back hard on mine and knew at once it was fairly hooked. The salmon held in the current about three feet down, shaking its head ponderously from side to side. There were vivid, important flashes of silver at least four feet long.

Out in the black water, no ordinary fish had taken. Minutes passed while the giant salmon writhed and turned. Terrified, I could think only of the utterly worthless leader.

For half an hour the salmon simply held in the current relatively unconcerned about the fact it was hooked. When I waded deep into the river to shorten the line and increase the pressure, the salmon drifted easily downstream gaining another hundred feet of line as it moved toward the far bank. There it surfaced, wallowing and twisting for fifteen or twenty minutes.

By now, well down in the pool with my fish, the others went on fishing in the riffle. I remember seeing someone with a fish on.

An hour later my salmon still seemed unconcerned, doing as it pleased, making no abrupt moves. Several curious fishermen gathered on the gravel bar to watch and offer encouragement.

I continued to wade into the river to minimize drag on the line. Putting on all the pressure possible, I held the rod flexibly to absorb sudden shocks, which the pitiful leader would never withstand.

A quarter of an hour later the salmon turned and began swimming steadily downstream. I backed out of the water and ran along the bank reeling furiously. It was nearing my side of the river and soon I was abreast, then ahead, pulling as hard as I dared. This would have been nearly the end for an ordinary forty-pounder. But this fish was just beginning to think it was in trouble and it turned sharply, swinging into midstream, taking back all the line I'd gained. Too big to get over into the next pool, it hung on the lip of the riffle.

"This could be the big one," Frank Bertaina observed quietly. And seeing there was really nothing he could do but offer pointless encouragement, he went back upstream to fish.

Shortly, the huge salmon began swimming deliberately toward the pool, stopping to shake its head every ten or fifteen yards, making the whole two hundred yards casually.

When it reached the pool it immediately turned and started down. Again I stayed in front, trying to lead it as close as possible. Again it swung out at the last minute to hold in midstream at the lip of the riffle.

The struggle was going into its second hour. My arms were tired and stiff and I was a nervous wreck. Far upstream I could see the little huddle of anglers still at their fishing.

The salmon hung suspended in the clear water for some minutes as it had before. Then I began to gain line. Inches at a time, backing went onto the spool. Ten minutes later the monofilament shooting line was in the guides and before long the shooting head itself was close to the rod tip. At this range the size of the fish was obvious.

John Bach was standing nearby. "Can I tail him?" he asked.

Normally, large fish can be led to the beach where the angler can gill them himself. But here the water was so shallow that the salmon could swim no closer than thirty or forty feet from shore.

"OK," I said to John, "if I can tip him over out there, see what you can do."

The salmon could scarcely negotiate in a foot and a half of water. It was a huge male, bright as they come, its dorsal fin and tail a soft pink, wavering out of water. My tiny blue fly was stuck clearly in the left corner of its mouth just below the dark eye, which seemed to look with contempt and defiance.

John took some tentative steps into the river. Frightened, the salmon bolted strongly away, taking back the several hundred feet of line just gained. I wondered if the salmon had let itself be drawn close merely out of curiosity.

I thought once more of the pathetic tippet, which was certainly on the verge of parting, and my confidence waned. That the fragile leader had held this long was nothing short of a miracle. My arms were nearly numb from two and a half hours of constant stress and I hoped I'd have the needed reflexes when the difficult finish was finally at hand. It seemed as I lost strength, the fish gained it.

Once again the arduous pumping of line began. This time I asked John to wade out into the water, crouch and wait motionless until the salmon was near him and on its side.

I knew I couldn't tire the massive fish with the feeble leader but I hoped to disorient it. The salmon was too big to be moved by main force even with a sound leader. The fish was a foot and a half thick and I hoped it would tilt over in a foot of water, giving John a chance.

Oddly, it came as planned, actually cruising at us half above water and I had to reel smartly to keep the line tight. Ten feet from where John was crouching, it grounded, keeled over on its side and began wallowing.

"Now! Can't move him any more." I urged John, forgetting all caution.

Then the leader broke. Instantly the salmon stopped struggling, righted itself and sat perfectly still. John and I were momentarily transfixed, then we lunged like madmen. An easy thrust of its tail moved it out of reach. Even as we thrashed toward it, the incredible king knew it was free, gathered speed as if it had never been hooked, and made a sizzling hundred-yard run that threw a wave clearly seen three hundred yards away.

I was tired, helpless and cleanly defeated as I admired what would have been the largest salmon ever captured on a fly rod swim back to rest once more in the greenest depths of the pool.

Bill Schaadt offered sympathy. "A shame. It was well up in the sixties. He was just too big, that's all."

That night I was home in San Francisco in the rain. I heard the river came up ten feet. Later, I called Jack Geib to see how it was dropping.

"Going down nicely. We'll be fishing again in a day or two." To which he added, "You might like to know that a bait fisherman caught a sixty-four-and-a-half-pounder above the forks yesterday and it had a fly in its mouth."

My feelings were definitely mixed. I wanted to believe that fish made it safely to the spawning grounds. The notion it had been killed by a treacherous hunk of its own kind's spawn seemed unfair.

On the other hand if the fly were mine I would know for sure the size of the monster I would never forget. I described the pattern to Jack but he was never able to see the fly, even though a bait fisherman did duly weigh and record a sixty-four-and-a-half-pounder which he had caught above the forks.

So I still believe in the immortality of that royal salmon, imagining it lived to reproduce its kind and provide a new generation of great fish to someday show another angler the strength of the king.

Chapter Ten

SMALL ODYSSEY*

You couldn't see them from above. Yet the steelhead were there, locked into special eddies of current, furling like so many flags in an easy breeze. This was the river of their ancestors, changed and controlled now, but still holding enough basic wildness to be rediscovered in successive moments of sensation and sexual inspiration. Not to mention just plain good luck.

* Copyright © 1976 by Time, Inc.

It had been three months since the great trout turned away from the sea in July. Now they were three hundred and fifty miles inland, crowding the Continental Divide where every arroyo was flushed with pure cadmium sumac and afternoon winds dispatched fallen leaves along the streambeds.

Soon these fish would find a winter resting pool then spawn in the spring. Most had become river rainbows again, their backs having turned from steel blue to olive, their sides from pure silver to deep red. They favored the edges of heavy water and boulder-strewn bottoms, places where an effortless sidling movement would put them immediately into the main flow where their sense of assurance was strongest.

Once in October an early storm gathered out of the northwest. The sky darkened and lowered, jamming itself against the mountains and a strong wind soughed through stands of fir, driving the first raindrops angularly into the forest. Sensing a change in pressure, the steelhead seemed to withdraw, settled deep in their lies, and would not move unnecessarily.

Caught in mindless service to the flow, the trout sensed nothing of the fly line curling slickly through the air nearby. Nor did they suspect the angler who stepped carefully along the shore a few yards away.

There was a bleakness in the river that tunneled their vision and dulled their spirit. This tyranny was reflected in prisms of gray light, shafts of gloom that barely reached the bottom. Hour after hour the fish dedicated themselves to nothing more than nosing the relentless current in a testament to pointlessness, instinct and cold blood.

Contrastingly, the fisherman concerned himself with every device at his command. He could not help thinking and among his many thoughts he was sure there was one, or a combination of several, which would help him catch a steelhead. As the wind blew harder through the canyon and sheets of rain slanted out of the darkening sky, he changed to a brighter fly and knew, even as he did so, that it was not the answer.

He considered: the Clearwater River in Idaho where he now fished—not an inconsequential stream, having gathered broadly out of the wilderness just west of Montana; the North Fork—cut off by monstrous Dworshak Dam only yards from its mouth, a dam with the clean appearance of finality, like a fiery auto wreck where you knew without a doubt the driver was dead; the North Fork's genetic strain of steelhead—truly large fish, comparable many felt, to those of the upper Skeena drainage in British Columbia; Dworshak Hatchery—a fifteen-million-dollar facility, the largest in the world devoted to the propagation of steelhead.

And he imagined: the implacable North Pacific Ocean—home to the steelhead during the years prior to their spawning journey, a dream of unknown voyages; imperceptible lunar forces, strange days beneath the polar ice cap; Astoria—where the particular water from a tributary in eastern Idaho was one part in one billion as the vast flow invited its offspring; the Columbia—Portland, broad farms, high desert and then the Snake River; the Clearwater itself—sometimes deep and still, sometimes wide and fast, always waiting.

And he remembered: other days, other places, other streams and wondered if anything was learned there; the particular tricks of angling—mending line to slow the drift, delicate, sparsely dressed flies, careful variation to cover all the water; advice—fish fast, move often; the preceding day—fishless, offering no clue, no moment of triumph or revelation, no advantage of having taken the first one.

And he saw the perfect steadiness of the river—turning

with complete lack of purpose, speaking a beautiful language that meant absolutely nothing; the gray sky—oppressive, like a room with a low ceiling, defying the sun; the rocks at his feet —green and moss-covered, growing darker until lost in the confused depths near, he knew, the heart of the mystery.

In deciding to go steelhead fishing during the fall he had had a choice of several rivers. There was the redoubtable Umpqua, for one, the most famous steelhead stream in the country since the time of Zane Grey. Or the North Fork of the Stillaguamish in Washington, or any one of numerous streams, like the Deschutes, which ran into the Columbia.

He had chosen the Clearwater first of all because of the size of its fish. One could almost expect a twenty-pounder and he knew some people thought the next world record would be caught there. The present record for the river is twenty-nine and a half, and larger ones have been reported, if not recorded.

And because of Dworshak Hatchery, which was expected to have more fish entering it than it could handle, fishing might be expected to be good. Then, too, the Clearwater steelhead were prime summer-run fish that rose eagerly to the fly and were noted for their determined battle.

He did not regret his choice. But as he struggled through each new riffle with the wind driving his best casts askew, he felt in a state of infancy and wondered more than ever how and why the great trout were caught.

He assumed the presence of fish and felt his methods were reasonably correct. But if the steelhead saw the odd flash of fly moving above them they never showed it.

Later that night as he tried to sleep, he felt helpless, and listening to the wind howl outside, only vaguely anticipated the dawn.

When the angler awoke in the morning it was quiet. The air stood light and different, the sky fragile and infinite. Sunlight struck the highest slopes and he instantly regretted not having risen earlier.

He decided upon a certain riffle that had attracted him earlier, and on the way there he passed a smooth run—one he'd fished the day before—where a fly-fisherman was fighting a steelhead. Moments later he arrived at a bridge where a spin fisherman was absurdly playing a fish from the high span.

He turned onto a dirt road that followed the river. Warm light flowed against the hills, and over the bright red sumac a covey of quail whirred. He thought what a good sign it was to have seen two fish on.

The riffle glittered magically, invitingly, as each little eddy and curl caught a particle of morning light, then swirled away beneath a faint mist of diamond dust. There was no breeze and the fisherman could see the beveled bottom near shore and foresaw the trajectory of his casts.

He pulled line from his reel and even these ratchety bursts were like a proclamation of faith. And the line slid through the air more smoothly than usual and the new fly, not really much different from yesterday's, looked somehow sleeker and better. And when he fished, his drift had something like moment in it that made him sure it was right.

Beneath the run itself uneven beams of yellow, red and orange flicked over the cobblestones and this new confection of light excited the steelhead. There was a certain lightness in their mood as they hung potently high in the water. Some swung widely from side to side often crossing the backs of others. Sometimes their white mouths showed momentarily, gaping nervously open then shut.

Occasionally, fish savagely inhaled small pieces of bark or

leaves which chanced to float near them. Several small trout hovered anxiously behind the bigger fish and once were chased many yards downstream by one of the steelhead.

A brilliant female lay forward of the rest. She was broad and heavy, her sides like mother-of-pearl. She held like a sentinel, challenging the river, the flickering sunlight. . . .

The angler cast quartering down, mended his line once, then waited tensely as his fly swung around. The cast was essentially no different from any other, over water much the same as that above and below. But when the tiny fly tilted into the steelhead's sight, she struck like a teased viper, sending a violent rush of water back among the other fish.

He saw the boil but there was simply no time to react and his line and flyless leader streamed loosely away in the current. Immediately the fish leaped high into the air, somersaulting back. Again it jumped, tail-walking sideways and he saw it framed against the willows on the far side. Finally, upstream, it came out in a long, graceful arc. He was stupified.

For a long time the fisherman sat dejected. Why me, he thought, but later began to see it as a success of sorts. After all, a fish did take the fly and had he perhaps been more alert it would now be lying on the bank beside him.

But even if the leader had held, he realized he still had no idea whatsoever why the fish had struck. It was all such a matter of open conjecture, all a guess, all a maelstrom of supposition. And all perfectly calculated to make him want to cast again and again.

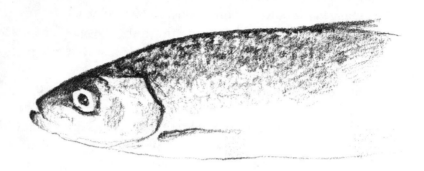

Chapter Eleven

HERRING IS BELIEVING

Dark clouds in the March sky fled south along the top of Inverness Ridge. In bleak reflection below, Tomales Bay reached out, embracing Hog Island, then making its way through treacherous narrows to meet the Pacific at the bottom of Bodega Bay's full curve.

The town of Point Reyes Station lies at the head of the bay

near Paper Mill Creek's estuary, and as I traveled toward it on State Highway 1 gusting winds pushed at the old Plymouth. It was no day to think of fishing. Even without harsh weather, March in California is a time of lull for the fly-caster. The steelhead season is closed in most rivers and where open it is apt to be unsuitable for fishing because of high water. Black bass are not yet fully active, the stripers remain in the turbid delta and the ocean is generally too rough for rockfishing. It is early for shad, and the trout season has not yet opened.

It was for these reasons as well as some others that I had planned a day of sketching. Several stops evolved: one near Nick's Cove, again at the Marshall Boat Works and finally close to the hamlet of Marshall itself, where an old hotel was worthy of attention. Everything seemed slowed under the dull sky before the promise of spring. Scoters and goldeneye ducks bobbed in the chop, an occasional gull swept overhead and bunches of mud hens lurched about absurdly on the exposed tidal flat behind Laughlin's store.

Presently, a field of motion in the sky north of Cypress Point caught my eye. It was a vague shimmer of confetti-like white particles, which through a pair of binoculars became a mass of wheeling gulls and pelicans. They had to be over herring, which could mean action, excitement—new life in the old day. The sketching had become troublesome anyway, progress at an impasse that only longer consideration in the studio could resolve. So paints and brushes went back into the box. A chance to play was at hand.

To get a closer look it was necessary to drive past the point toward Blake's Landing. As the road skirted a low bluff, there was a place to pull the car over, walk to the edge and survey the scene. Below and for great distances right and left a melee of little Bonaparte's gulls hovered and danced in groups like marionettes whose strings converged underwater rather than overhead. Higher, pelicans soared, veered, then dived with military precision. The herring were being driven within reach of the birds by any number of sea lions charging through the schools, scattering the little fish like sparks from a grinding wheel.

An otherwise gloomy day had been brought to life by moments reminiscent of those past, when striped bass had been caught amid such turmoil. Time and place changed to become the Gulf Stream, then lower Baja. The fish, unseen beneath the glare, could have been some voracious pelagic species available to the reckless angler. Reality returns. Back here on Tomales Bay, how can some fishing be made out of this?

Herring do provide a certain sport. Their appearance in San Francisco Bay, especially along the Sausalito waterfront and in Tomales Bay between Marconi and Miller Park, routs many families out of the house and to the shore for Sunday outings. At Tomales such forays are often combined with cockle digging at low water, shell collecting and picnicking. This family fishing is generally done with a variety of nets, many of ingenious design, or with treble hooks that are cast and then retrieved fast through a school, snagging the herring.

On weekends a large gallery of spectators forms to watch the ritual of the herring run in Sausalito. Tired of seeing endless pounds of the sterling little fish come ashore by the net and bucketful, one may retire to a nearby pub or turn attention to the passing stream of humanity. Bridgeway Street will be choked to a crawl with a succession of Porsches and Fords and families from Des Moines mingling with a counter-culture that still believes less is more.

One may also find time to pity the poor herring—the universal hors d'oeuvre. Found throughout the oceans of the world in one form or another, it provides forage for innumerable large species of fish as well as for birds and sea lions. Even the eggs, when spawned upon rocks, pilings and seaweed, are eaten by gulls as the tide recedes. Then there are the tons of fish that are netted each year for commercial use. Many fishermen have observed a decline in the number of herring along the California coast. This is a serious matter to anglers, the herring being a primary source of food for big-game fish such as striped bass and Pacific salmon.

While standing at my vantage point on the bluff, none of the protective considerations entered my mind. Angling did. A search of the car's trunk turned up a fly rod and a reel spooled with a Dacron line. It was a steelhead outfit and too heavy for catching ten-inch fish under ordinary circumstances but it would do just fine on this blowy day. Some small silver shad flies, dug up from under the debris in the glove compartment, completed the rig.

Thus prepared, I slid down the bank, climbed out on a rock and made a tentative cast. Something tapped the fly immediately. Then came a steady pull, not heavy but the fish was courageous in its struggle, and I had my first fly-caught herring. They hit readily and jumped better than trout, more like the minuscule tarpon they are. Not only was catching them fun, but the whole scene was alive with the action of nature. Just the sounds alone were as consuming as a river rapid that merges all into one song. The steady north wind rhythmically pushed wavelets against shore while gulls screamed and sea lions barked. Then, quite suddenly, the wind picked up and the day turned even colder. It became difficult to cast, so I quit, content with the unexpected fishing.

Like shad, herring run earlier at the southern end of their range, near San Francisco, and later in the north along Alaska's shores. And the weather is not always as bleak as it was that day. Along the Pacific coast, especially in northern California, there are many beautiful days throughout winter and spring. Herring enter San Francisco Bay as early as the end of November but may not spawn until January, February or March. There are usually some in Tomales Bay by December, precipitating an occasional heavy feeding spree among the local striped-bass population.

But March is the best month. This is when spawning activity is near its peak and the weather is apt to be pleasant. In size the fish will vary from eight to twelve inches, larger than the average put-and-take trout found in California streams. In areas where growth is rapid, as in some parts of Alaska, herring often exceed a pound, which means about eighteen inches in length.

Plankton eaters, herring respond best to flies with glitter rather than those designed to be some particular food imitation. I have caught them on size 14 hooks to size 4, though the smaller sizes are best for obvious reasons.

The water near shore is usually less than six feet deep, so it is possible to cast to an area where fish are to be seen dimpling the surface; the fly is retrieved without bothering to let it sink. The most suitable tackle is the same as for small trout. It is the fishing, not the fighting of the fish, that is the point, but light tackle is most appropriate just the same. There will be no tangling with lunkers; line will not be stripped from a screaming reel.

In pursuit of larger, more difficult game, a different dimension of sport arises, one that certainly provides excitement but also implies competition, if not with other anglers, then with the powerful quarry itself. When the prey is as small as a herring there can be only the purest—and hardly insignificant—fishing moments.

Man has responded to the salmon runs, from earliest times, with a sense of wonder and gratitude that adds to his own stature; and each new understanding of their sensitivity and complexity expands him and enhances his concept of the world that sustains him and, thus far, tolerates him.

RODERICK L. HAIG-BROWN*

---

* Roderick Haig-Brown is an author living in the town of Campbell River on Vancouver Island. He is the magistrate for that district as well as chancellor of the University of British Columbia. You could probably get a consensus that Haig-Brown is the finest living angling writer in the English language. *The Western Angler, Return to the River, A River Never Sleeps, Fisherman's Fall,* are just a few of his works that are regarded as classics.

Chapter Twelve

A SOMETIME ISLAND OF DREAMS

It is an evening like autumn itself; a break, simple definition, a capsule moment of change that states a promise.

Blue dusk, and a grassy incline ending abruptly against cobblestones at the edge of the Nimpkish River. The impression is without detail and very still: slope of forest beyond the stream, suggestive darkness where woods and water meet, and the last daylight caught on edges of current; sky, spun slowly away into shadow.

The brisk air of early fall is a sharp, moist presence. An eagle cuts it slowly, down the canyon's draft, swinging easily into high branches. Also without hurry, the river slides beneath the eagle's eye toward nearby Queen Charlotte Strait along the eastern edge of Vancouver Island.

Nearby stand the last untended trees of a small apple orchard. The ground has been manicured into a campground giving it the vague appearance of an English garden. In a moment of *déjà vu* I know where I am: through the twilight I imagine the primrose yellow farmhouse set near a hedgerow of chokecherry. With somewhat more immediacy I picture the Lansdowne Pool beyond the clearing, flowing hard against the far bank.

The homestead and river are for an instant, as they were when Haig-Brown described them so many years ago in *A River Never Sleeps.*

In the darkening corridor along the stream I see several ponderous wakes pushing lines of light with varying and uncertain speed. Salmon!

Francis Golden, a fellow artist, and I spent the previous evening on the spit at Campbell River, watching the trollers work the tide in Discovery Passage. It seemed an uninteresting occupation, a nice boat ride spoiled, in fact. Besides, we were looking for a place to fly-fish.

At dark I telephoned Mr. Haig-Brown. Within the hour we were seated in his comfortable study.

At one point I asked about the Campbell, and Haig-Brown led us outside, across the lawn to where the river rushed by. The Campbell is now controlled by a dam and flows unnaturally, rising and dropping in accordance with valves and switches—deeply heartbreaking to those who sense the value of a river. We lingered there, unable to really see anything and I understood the only thing still truly free and wild about the Campbell was its mercurial sound.

Back inside, Haig-Brown commented, "Should be tyees in the Nimpkish. They're hard to cover off your feet, but look at the Lansdowne Pool. Fish will wait there for a freshet."

At daylight the sky is clear and little whorls of fog hang in certain pockets among the trees and along the river. Upstream is a wooded island and a steep riffle, above which the tide no longer has any effect. The current enters the pool at an angle, pushes over against a rock bank, then spreads back into a deep lie.

In waders there is only one place we can reach any kind of good water at all and that's near the riffle. The best holding water, which is the deep basin in the center of the pool, is much too far away to cover.

This morning there is a high tide and we fish intermittently throughout the falling water but catch nothing and see only a few scattered rolls, mostly very low in the pool.

However, on the ebb tide, fish begin showing steadily in a confined area over the deepest water. They're not big, but right now we won't be terribly choosy. It occurs they might be reached from the other side.

Some distance downstream there is a place where I barely manage to wade the river even at low tide. Frank decides to stay on the near side and is becoming understandably discouraged about our chances.

Over on the deep side things still don't look good. Initially, I find the upper end of the pool is not as deep as I'd assumed.

Then, with the sun slanting into the clear water I can plainly see there are no fish in it. We have spent the morning casting at nothing.

Fish continue rolling in the center of the pool but with trees and a high bank at my back I'm forced to roll cast, and the seventy feet I barely manage is not enough by a full thirty more.

The fish change their demeanor: the earlier splashy rolls become slow porpoise-like moves. In salmon this is often an indication they are ready to grab but since I can't reach these fish I can't find out.

As I watch, seeing the individual fish more clearly, I wonder if perhaps many of them are just stragglers from earlier runs of pink or chum salmon. I ask myself, too, how many there really are. Are most of them rolling or only a small percentage?

If the sun were still on the water I would climb the high bank and simply look into the pool but it is now late afternoon and the water is in deep shadow. And no matter how many fish there are, the situation is completely hopeless without a boat.

"Maybe there's a place to go trout fishing around here," suggests Frank.

But I argue that we haven't yet made a single real fishing cast into the pool. I'm sure there are no kings in yet but feel the tidewater situation makes the river very viable and that conditions can change radically overnight. We decide to spend the night and if things look promising the next day, we'll go into town and hire a small boat.

In the morning I walk to the stream and within ten minutes four big bright fish roll thunderously. It's hard to tell what they might be exactly but they were not there the day before, which means a school of new fish moved in during the high tide before dawn.

I insist on trying for the boat so we drive to town where we soon learn there are absolutely none for rent. Furthermore, the local people tell us the great Nimpkish runs of thirty years ago have been wiped out. They add that even if the river turns black with salmon we won't catch any because salmon won't take a fly. And if we are fool enough to try and a big king accidentally gets on the line, we will sorely regret it because our tackle will be smashed.

"Let's go trout fishing," Frank pleads.

"No."

There are five distinctly different species of Pacific salmon in North America and the assortment of local names by which each is known creates some confusion about this. For example, I met an old commercial fisherman on the Nimpkish and asked him how the run of tyees was, thinking I'd avoid being taken for a complete tourist by calling the fish its proper local name.

"Tyees!" he said impatiently. "You mean springs don't you? Tyee's a handle them sports down at Campbell River tacked on 'em."

The largest salmon of all is most widely called the king. These fish average between fifteen and thirty pounds with many running forty or fifty. The largest ever captured was slightly over a hundred and twenty-five pounds.

In the Columbia River they are called chinooks and in British Columbia are referred to as either tyees or springs. In California, Oregon, Washington and Alaska they are kings and I always refer to them as such because the name is perfectly descriptive.

The silver salmon, averaging eight or ten pounds, and as

popular a game fish as the king, is also widely known as the coho.

Sockeyes, a very important commercial species, are sometimes called reds, and around the Columbia River are also known as bluebacks. A pink salmon and a humpback are one and the same fish as is the chum and dog salmon.

The situation is muddled further by the percentage of one-year-old precocious kings and silvers, which often lead their respective runs up the rivers. These fish may weigh from one to about eight pounds and are almost invariably males called jacks, chubs or grilse. They evidently represent a biological safeguard should a female find herself on the redd without a large male to fertilize her eggs. As with all animals, normally the males fight among themselves for the privilege of being with the female and these little fish are driven away. But they are fertile, should their presence be needed.

These immature fish die after ascending their river whether they actually spawn or not as does every other Pacific salmon. Biologically, the reason for this is that in preparation for spawning, salmon undergo an irreversible physiological change in their digestive systems. In short, it becomes impossible for them to utilize food.

A distinction should be made between salmon and steelhead, which are actually sea-run rainbow trout. Steelhead do not necessarily die after spawning but may return several years in succession.

Frank and I would be happy to catch any of the five kinds of salmon and certainly steelhead too, if we could find any, imposing only two conditions upon our efforts: we wished to fly-fish and preferred to do so in a river, any river.

We had taken the ferry from Kelsey Bay to Beaver Cove which is only minutes from the Nimpkish. Golden is delightfully gregarious and while on the boat became involved in conversation with a man who was the self-proclaimed wizard of hunting and fishing on Vancouver Island.

With his head cocked smartly to one side he had informed Frank, "Only a cripple or an idiot could starve here!" Then had gone on to demand, "Now, just what *do* you want to fish for?"

"We're going to fly-fish for salmon," Frank answered innocently. "In a river."

"Hope you don't plan on catching any," the man sneered, "because they don't take flies in fresh water."

Frank looked pretty worried and glanced desperately at me. I shrugged, not wishing to argue, and stepped out on deck. We were moving through a strait bordered on the west by a steep bevel of mountain which disappeared upward into the overcast. A killer whale surfaced ahead, its long dorsal fin vanishing implacably in a slow arc. An immense slick remained and as the boat passed I wondered if he'd take a fly.

I thought of our wizard and his agressive disinterest in fly-fishing for salmon. In this, I realized, he was not alone. During the preceding month I'd assembled a preposterous phone bill in an effort to gather a little information. Most people I'd talked to simply said flatly that salmon wouldn't take a fly after entering fresh water. I was astonished further at the firm, almost universal lack of curiosity in the matter.

The salmon's willingness to take our flies was not debatable as far as I was concerned. Frank could not have a very determined opinion about it because he'd never fished for salmon or steelhead before. He would have to rely heavily on my judgment and ability, which at the moment remained entirely open to question.

One thing I knew for sure: the problem was not going to

be that salmon wouldn't take flies. The trick would be finding a river suitable for fly-fishing that also had schools of resting fish in it.

Just out of Port McNeill we stopped at Cluxewe Beach where the silvers might have been running. Unfortunately, the weather had turned blustery and a strong south wind laced up the strait putting fishing out of the question, so we decided to go inland.

On the road to Port Alice we got our first real look at the altogether appalling destruction of the island through a program of logging that is more deeply ruthless than anything of its kind I have ever seen. Literally every possible flat and lower slope was clear-cut, leaving a tragic vista of stumps and slash.

Everywhere smoke billowed forth indicating the remains of fires set to burn old slash and in several instances smoke was pouring out of high, green timber where the set fires had gotten out of control.

The landscape had the look of another planet—or perhaps our own, only after some monstrous holocaust. Over the years the lumber industry has gripped the island the way an owl holds a rodent. The capture was silent, made in inaccessible territory where few eyes could see it, and it may well be permanent, just as the mouse must remain in unretractable talons until it is eaten.

Certainly at one time, the island, its rivers and the surrounding sea represented one of the most superb interdependent ecosystems on earth. It may not be out of line to say that the destruction of Yellowstone Park would be a crime less grave.

Aside from the fact the logging companies control the roads over much of the island, their supreme industrial arro-

gance seemed perfectly stated by a large Kwakiutl Bear Pole
near the road at the Nimpkish River.

Along with three or four loads of buckshot at close range,
the pole bore a bronze plaque which read as follows:

KWAKIUTL BEAR POLE
by Mr. Jack James of Kwicksustaineux
Indian Band at Simoon Sound, B.C.
To commemorate the Centenary of
the union in 1866 of the colonies on
Vancouver Island and the mainland
as British Columbia.
LOG DONATED BY MACMILLAN, BLOEDEL
AND POWELL RIVER LIMITED.

Eventually we drop into a canyon where there is a wooden
bridge with a small sign reading MARBLE RIVER. To our left is
a lake, from which the river flows, and below the bridge there
is a pool. We are under a thick pall of orange smoke and
after the devastation through which we've just driven, I have
little hope there will be any fish.

As we cross the bridge I see rings dissipating on the pool
and mention it to Frank. We stop, walk back for a look and
are almost unable to grasp the scene.

The hole is perhaps a hundred feet wide and two or three
times as long. In the center where the deep water begins, fish
obscure the bottom. Below us they are milling so thickly they
resemble worms in a can. These I identify as salmon, probably kings. At least two dozen enormous steelhead are lying at
the tail of the pool in precise formation against the current.

I begin screaming at Frank, who raises his arm for protection as he backs cautiously away. But immediately I change
my attitude to one of quiet resignation.

"It's Sunday," I say with a perverted smile and simple gesture of hand. "And obviously this water is closed to fishing or else the pool would be ringed with people lobbing spoons. We'll stroll back to the car and look it up. You'll see."

We look it up and the water is not closed to fishing. Frank again recoils in fear as I burst out, sending a shower of tackle all over the ground.

"I want to take some pictures," Frank says cautiously.

"Fine, fine."

"Do you think we can catch any?"

"Is there a mustache in Mexico? Hurry up!"

The water is extremely clear and I keep a low profile creeping into position beneath the bridge. Across the river Frank is down among some bushes with a telephoto lens.

"OK?" I call.

"Ready."

The first cast falls short because I am testing backcast room. The next extends flatly behind me then flies straight across, and the tiny blue fly turns over without complication two feet from the rocks.

I let the Dacron line settle about six feet then begin to retrieve. Instantly the line pulls away and I'm on a hot, bright fish that dashes downstream jumping end over end. It's a small king about eight pounds which jumps once more quite close before throwing the hook.

Frank abandons his bushes, comes around and slides down the bank behind me with his fly rod. I urgently motion him over but before he can even get started I notice something glinting up above.

"Uh oh," I nod.

"What?"

"Look up on the bridge."

"Wait a minute. They can't do that. Can they?" Frank is incensed.

"Can and will."

Above us a man in a silver hard hat is looking with amazement at the water. With him are his wife and two daughters. All are armed with stout spinning rods fitted with spoons resembling heavy-duty shoehorns. Simultaneously they let fly. Four large boulders thrown in among the fish would have had the same effect. It was over.

Frank was gagging. "I came all the way from Connecticut . . ."

We decide to walk downstream.

"Maybe the whole river is like this!" I offer excitedly. "The fish part I mean."

But it isn't. Below the bridge are a series of spectacular falls. The pockets below each are full of resting salmon and steelhead. It is a place where no fishing of any kind should ever be allowed as evidenced by the fact any number of people there are hard at work snagging with spinning rods and large spoons.

In the white water of the falls, steelhead are leaping frantically only to be thwarted by high rock. Occasionally a fish makes it over, swimming with almost impossible speed, strength and determination.

Below this it is a superb stream, although we don't find many fish. We meet another fly-fisherman who is carrying a six-pound steelhead but it is the only one he's taken in two days.

"Have you seen many salmon?" I ask.

"Salmon? Some, but they won't take a fly you know."

It is late afternoon when we go back to the bridge wondering how it might be. Five or six families are picnicking at the nearby campground. Children scamper all over, throwing rocks in the water. Two boys are sitting on the bridge dangling spoons. Below them a logger is casting a rigged herring.

But the *pièces de résistance* are the skin divers. Dressed in black wet suits, flippers, face masks and snorkels, they are cavorting in the middle of the hole. We utter a moan of sympathy for the fish. Those not darting aimlessly in panic are huddled in deep water against the bridge pilings.

It is cocktail hour.

We spend the night and when I wake up at dawn, I decide to give the pool an early try. On the first cast I catch a small king. But after that, nothing, and I am not particularly surprised recalling yesterday's catastrophe.

Frank is watching from up on the bridge and I ask him how the fish are responding to my fly.

"They're scared to death of it."

A van stops on the bridge, a man gets out and, seeing me fishing, asks, "Any good?"

"Nope."

"Salmon," he says, shaking his head. "Salmon won't bite flies. What you need is a buzz bomb."

"That right?"

"Buzz bomb 'em, that's what I do. Give 'em the ole buzz bomb."

I reel in and meet Frank on his way back to the car.

"What the hell is a buzz bomb?" he asks.

"Damned if I know."

"Let's get out of here. How about some trout fishing?"

The weather turns clear and calm. With a high tide at noon there is still a chance of seeing silvers at Cluxewe Beach so we go there.

We are standing near the car, putting our equipment together, when a sedan careens out of the trees into the clearing and skids to a stop nearby. There are two men in it and they both have rifles.

Rolling down a window, the first demands seriously, "Seen any bears?"

"No," we reply, not ever having thought to look.

Both men eye us for long moments. I wonder if they think we are hiding something. Then the man at the window changes his tone knowingly. "Oh, you must *just* be fishermen."

I am startled after the men leave to come upon fresh bear tracks nearby. There are also piles of fresh dung composed entirely of vivid blueberries.

"Hey Frank, look at this."

"Yeh, now if I could see blue bear dung and cohos in the same day I'd really have it made."

The strait is calm and the tide nearly in. Two salmon jump right away but too far out. Another fly-caster arrives and the three of us sit on an old log watching the water.

We see a seal surface twice and the third time he has a salmon in his mouth. Some say seals scare the fish, others feel it's a good sign to see them because it means there are fish around.

Suddenly, a small fish jumps no more than fifty feet away and the three of us wade in and start to cast. The other fisherman hooks a coho—possibly the one that jumped—and in a few minutes lands a five-pounder. But it is the only action during the next hour and a half.

Frank is ready for a sandwich and I agree to join him in a few minutes. When I do he is down on a grassy bank, casting into an estuary behind the spit. When he sees me he waves.

"Some kind of fish are jumping," Frank says quickly. "A man I just talked to told me there are Dolly Varden trout here."

Fish are surfacing in a very slow head and tail roll, reminding me exactly of nymphing brown trout.

"What do you think?" Frank asks.

"I have no idea. All we can do is fish carefully and maybe we'll catch one."

I watched Frank cast to no avail.

"They're just not biting."

"I don't know," I urge. "The tide's running out and maybe a particular water stage will excite them. Keep trying."

Meanwhile I sneak downstream trying to see what sort of water the fish are lying in. I dare not approach too closely for the water is crystal clear and I find out, shallow as well.

"You try it," Frank insists. "I'm going to go and get a sandwich."

In deference to the water, I replace the fly with a small number ten and lenghten the leader to about fifteen feet, tuning it down to six pound.

Three conditions are in our favor: the light is hazy, there is a slight breeze that crinkles the surface and the tide is moving well.

The fish continue rolling. I cast at an angle far downstream and retrieve slowly, bringing the fly up and into them.

After about thirty casts the line tightens slowly and a distinct pulse immediately tells me one of the fish has taken.

"Frank!"

Whatever it is it's very game. Its fight reminds me of that of the coho as it streaks along just beneath the surface, twists and makes several good jumps. I slide it up on the grass as Frank arrives with camera in hand.

"It's a pink, Frank. Look how beautiful it is!" Affectionately called humpies because of the formation on their backs during spawning, pinks have a very distinctive appearance. It is not at all homely as one is led to believe. Instead, the fish has tremendous character and a very singular image.

And the color! Radiant as mother-of-pearl: the eye is brilliant cadmium yellow complemented beneath by the cheeks which are clear turquoise blue. The gills are tinged a delicate pink and the black spots on the tail are an unusual oblong shape, unlike those of any other salmon. The belly is pure white, changing below the lateral line to olive, in a definite, jagged pattern.

"Here, you fish," I say to Frank, explaining where I got my strike. "They may go on the grab. The tide is right."

Taking the rod, Frank casts and instantly has a fish on. I'm enjoying taking pictures.

"This is my first salmon!" he yells sternly. "My first salmon. Do you understand!"

He plays it well and it isn't an easy fish to beach, especially on the light leader. When landed, it is a male at least eight pounds, which is quite large for a pink.

In the next hour I land four more, all the same size as the first, about five pounds. The tide is now low and Frank determines to walk out past the end of the long point and gather some fresh clams for supper. I can't tear myself away from the pinks, now rolling six and eight at a time.

They are thick enough that if I am not careful I'll snag them accidentally. I find by standing directly uptide so line and fly travel parallel to them, I avoid this problem entirely. Sometimes they swim into the line anyway but I simply let it go and they swim away.

The bite is truly on. Fishing acquires the feeling of dance, with the salmon showing slowly, rhythmically. I try for precision of cast; roll, one backcast and a strait turnover. I am in a trance.

I have a fish on all the time for at least three hours. They are not particularly hard to land though they are fast. One curious detail is their slim, seemingly weak mouth. I find I must use special care in releasing them. If I could describe the pink in a word it would be: delicate.

The man who'd been casting off the beach comes down and sees me fishing.

"Those are just old dogs in there," he confides. "They won't take anything, not even spoons."

I hook one, bring it to the beach and release it. He is astonished.

"You mean it actually bit?"

"Biting like I've never seen. Caught twenty, maybe twenty-five. There's room here, why don't you fish?"

"Oh, no thanks. I'm going upstream and see if there are any trout."

The next morning fishing is just as good. We expand our operation a little and catch quite a few in several other tidewater pools of the Cluxewe River. We also take several sea-run cutthroat and a small Dolly Varden. We turn them all back.

"Say, Frank, remember that guy who was fishing off the beach yesterday? He came down last night and saw me into the pinks. Didn't phase him. Must be a little light in his loafers. Went upstream to look for trout."

"I can understand that." Frank smiles.

"You know what that's like? That's like going to a party where an orgy is in progress, having a gorgeous woman ask if there's anything she can do for you and you ask her where they're dunking for apples."

In the afternoon we must start back to Victoria. When we come to the bridge at the Nimpkish River there are several people standing on it looking into the water. We park and walk over.

Below is a school of at least thirty steelhead, easily averaging ten or twelve pounds. They swim nervously and with a clear sense of urgency, back and forth along the shadow of the bridge. They seem reluctant to pass under.

The men run back to their car to get rods and tackle boxes, telling their wives to keep an eye on the fish. When they return, the first man pulls out a package of herring and begins to unwrap it.

"They're feeding on top. Should be no trouble at all. Damn herring are still frozen . . ."

A third man has parked his car and comes out to look. His attitude is superior.

"That herring is no good," he warns the first man. "These fish aren't feeding. Use a spoon."

"Well, I've already got the . . ."

"You see," he insists, "the cutthroats follow the salmon up and hit them on the belly, causing eggs to drop out and they eat them. The salmon think the spoon is a trout and want to get even by killing it."

"Oh."

In spite of this advice the first man lowers his herring into the water where it slowly spins absurdly in the current. When the steelhead chance to swim near, they veer off sharply, alarmed by the giant bait.

The second man sees the wisdom in the third's advice so he

digs in his tackle chest and comes up with an immense silver cod jig, the closest thing he can find to a spoon.

Poised, he waits for the fish to pass. When they are right beneath him he fires his piece of steel straight down on top of them. Like a pinwheel, the fish scatter in complete panic, leaving great heaves in the surface of the water. The third man grunts, "Hunh."

"I really doubt these fish would hit anything anyway," I say idly.

"You could bottom-bump!" the third man says to me with anger in his voice.

Frank chimes in immediately, "We got any bottom-bumping equipment?"

Finally the steelhead manage to regroup themselves and after nosing the shadow again, swim quickly under the bridge and disappear upstream.

All the people go to their cars and drive away.

Frank and I stand for a while in the warm afternoon. The river is slick and streamers of moss wave in its current. We see eagles circling high overhead.

Then another big school of steelhead appears. And another. And another. And another. All behave the same: they are afraid of the bridge's shadow and nose it tentatively before darting under. Upstream, their wakes can be seen clear to the bend.

As we leave I think of the Lansdowne Pool and wonder if the steelhead will rest there this evening.

Chapter Thirteen

TO CATCH A STEELHEAD

Steamboat: strange name for a place where it would seem there never have been or ever will be any steamboats. But Steamboat, Oregon, while not noted for those redoubtable craft, is famous for steelhead. In fact, the thirty-odd-mile section of water on the North Umpqua, which is restricted to the use of flies, offers what is perhaps the best summer steelhead fly-fishing in the United States today.

Novelist William Hjortsberg, John Bailey and I had decided to fish the river for a few days late one summer. We'd driven from our homes in Livingston, Montana, to Hosmer Lake just outside Bend to fish for the Atlantic salmon found there. We took a number of these by sight fishing, much as one would on Salt-water flats casting for visible tarpon or bonefish. But after several days the weather turned cold and strong winds drove snow and sleet across the lake, so we decided to repair to a lower elevation. Since we were so close to the Umpqua, and neither William nor John had steelhead-fished much before, we elected to go over and try it.

We made the drive from Bend past Diamond Lake amid rain showers, hail, snow and patches of encouraging blue. In the upper canyon of the Umpqua, magnificent rainbows spanned impressive chasms of fir. Then, as we approached Steamboat Creek in the late afternoon, the sun came fully out and the sky was clear and unbroken.

I asked John to pull over at a place called Log Hole. Since I was the only one among us who'd fished the river previously, I'd have to be the guide though my own knowledge of the river could best be described as sketchy. I was delighted not to see another angler there ahead of us, and as we stood in the last rays of early evening sun admiring the deep emerald glide below, a great steelhead rolled in the pool.

I became hysterical. . . . Meanwhile John and William calmly assembled their equipment, not fully realizing I suppose, that we were going to *catch* that fish!

Since William was less familiar with steelhead fishing and also with long-distance casting than either John or I, and this fish could be covered with only about fifty feet of line, I asked John if he minded if William worked the fish first, and he said, no, he'd fish the lower end. So, after scrambling down the bank I explained briefly to William the standard way of covering steelhead when they roll and how to mend the line and then retrieve the fly in front of the fish. As his third cast swung through the best water his line drew forward and he brought the rod up sharply.

"I've got him!" he cried, a look of astonishment on his face. But before he could get the fish on the reel the hook pulled out.

"What happened?" he asked dejectedly. "He felt so heavy, like hooking a log." The only comment I could offer was that sometimes they just come off, small consolation to a man who's just lost his first steelhead.

We fished a while longer but it didn't seem like anything else was going to happen so we drove to the Wright Creek Pool. Since William had already hooked a fish we agreed that John should have the best water at the tail of the hole. I walked up to the middle and William looked on. There wasn't any backcast room here but since I was using a shooting head I could roll cast about eighty feet, which was far enough to cover the good water. Shortly, I had a very hard take that parted the leader. At the same instant I saw John come up on a fish downstream but it unhooked itself at once. We fished until dark without any more luck, then headed upstream to make camp.

Our conversation that evening centered around the fact that everything about the river seemed so fine. Our delight was essentially due to the fact that while throughout the country, and perhaps the world, natural resources such as rivers full of steelhead are on the decline, here was one on the ascent. And it's true that today the Umpqua offers better fishing than ever, thanks to the concerted efforts of many, not the least of whom is Frank Moore, owner of the Steamboat

Inn. He and a group of anglers and conservationists called the Steamboaters have pressed for improved logging practices with the hope of increasing the number of wild fish that are able to spawn naturally in the tributary streams.

A stocking program was initiated because thoughtless logging practices had destroyed the once labyrinthine spawning grounds. Now, as this problem is gradually corrected, it is hoped that the number of stocked fish can be reduced as the population of wild fish grows.

Some say the stocked fish are inferior to their wild counterparts but I'm inclined to disagree. Such notions must be based in part upon anglers' observance of a particular fish's fighting qualities and, as such, seem nebulous and subjective. Fly-fishermen are notoriously sentimental and any of us would prefer to *think* we are catching a wild fish rather than a planted one. But consider this: how can a fish that has made his way 100 miles down a river to the ocean, then spent two to four years traveling 1,000 to 2,500 miles, possibly to the north coast of the Asian Continent, and then course unerringly back to that same river, ascended the torturous 100 miles to the point of his birth and finally seized an angler's fly, be inferior? As far as I'm concerned, it can't.

Besides, any fish taken in the Steamboat area of the Umpqua is going to be inferior if you choose to look at it that way. After all, they're a hundred miles from the sea and many of the fish will be caught from four to twelve weeks after they've entered the river. Hook the same fish a mile out of the salt when he's only been in a few hours and he'll be a different animal. But this is far from the point. It's the excitement of the take that thrills the fly-fisherman and the Umpqua fish are avid hitters. What's more, they're *there*. You can't catch what's not there and the angler who complains of too many fish simply hasn't thought it through.

In keeping with the spirit of this singular river, anglers should be encouraged to release the majority of their fish. Few of the steelhead are in prime eating condition and will ultimately prove to be of greater value back in the water than in the frying pan. Present bag limits are two fish a day, six in possession and forty for the season. It would seem that no one needs to kill six steelhead today let alone forty. The fun of catching them should be enough.

The North Umpqua offers many kinds of water and angling situations. Frank Moore likes to fish in the rarest way of all, with a dry fly. And there's water for it. There are pools suitably fished with double tapers, weight forward lines and shooting heads. Floater, sinking tip, Dacron, high-density-plastic and lead-core lines may all be plied to advantage somewhere. There are riffles, runs, ledges, pools and pockets all of which hold fish at one time or another. There is a time and place for number-ten flies and for outsized 1/o's.

Oddly enough, over the years steelhead fishing has been fraught with superstition. It wasn't too many years ago winter fishermen on the coast would tell you flatly that steelhead wouldn't take a fly. Vestiges of some of the myths remain, particularly in regard to flies and how these should be retrieved or manipulated. For example, the first time I fished the Umpqua I was with two friends, Bob Tusken and Rudi Ferris. We were told categorically that Umpqua River steelhead wouldn't take a retrieved fly. Also that they would only hit certain few patterns. Our first day out we substantiated our contention that this was a preposterous notion by beaching eight steelhead all on flies dissimilar to anything used locally and fished with a rapid retrieve. The misconception that a fly must be drifted dead to interest a steelhead is perhaps based on the fact that in some kinds of water and under certain unusal circumstances steelhead may *not* take a fast-moving fly. Fishing a fly drag free is a popular method along Atlantic salmon streams and many traditionalists have applied the system to steelhead fishing. It's interesting to note that Ray Bergman, whose book *Trout* is probably among the most widely read angling books of this century, suggests floating the fly on a dead drift as an alternative to the ordinary way of fishing. Most of the time retrieving is best because you cover more water that way.

Insofar as flies are concerned, my choice for steelhead fishing is the comet type. I've always had good luck on the Umpqua, especially with those most sparsely dressed. Comets are extremely practical, combining ease of construction, good fishing qualities (they don't spin or flutter during the cast, they ride upright in the water and have an interesting undulating action all their own) and aesthetic appeal.

The method for fishing a holding spot might go something like this: starting as far upstream as seems right, work through the water with a sparse fly. The stream is normally extremely clear, which is the reason for the sparse dressing. If no fish are hooked on the first pass, go through again with a slightly more subdued fly, perhaps blue or green. Failing at this, remove the number four or six and try a number eight of some sort. If that doesn't work, abandon the pool and fish elsewhere. The exception would be if the fish were rolling continuously or you could see a large number of them from up above, then it would make sense to continue fishing the spot after further refining the tackle.

Generally speaking, steelhead are school fish so you're not just going to be fishing for one fish. Casting to just one or two can prove to be a long drawn-out procedure, so it seems

smarter to keep trying new water in the hope of finding a con-
centration to work over. Then, once such a situation is found
the problem becomes one of "tuning down" and staying with
it. Longer, lighter leaders, smaller flies and varied retrieves are
part of it.

One day during the trip with John and William we were
all fishing a certain pool. There was no doubt it held steelhead. After fishing through it using number fours without any
luck, I put on a number eight and caught a fish right away.
After that we hooked a couple more but then nothing. Later,
John and William decided to fish a few spots up the river and
I elected to remain where I was. There were plenty of steelhead around and if they ever decided to bite I'd be in business.
Toward the latter part of the afternoon something began to
happen. In the area of the pool where the greatest number of
fish would be apt to hold, steelhead began to roll.

I walked to the spot and made a cast upstream from the
last fish to show. As my fly passed the spot I had him. It was a
strong fish, about ten pounds, and took me some distance
down into the pool. Occasionally during the fight, which
lasted about ten minutes, I'd glance up the pool and see fish
rolling. I beached my steelhead, released it then walked back
upriver. Tying on a new fly, this time a blue comet, I began
fishing just below where I'd hooked the previous fish. Within
three casts I was tight to another. This one cartwheeled down
the pool making four or five end over end leaps until it was a
hundred and fifty feet away, but before I could follow, the
hook pulled out. As I was regaining line to start fishing again,
a fish showed above me. I waded out, walked the twenty feet
upstream, again tied on another fly—this time a number-eight
green one—made the cast and had him immediately. This fish
was beached in about a minute. It was scarred and cut as if

from a net and I wondered that it was still alive.

After releasing it I was back in the water, this time with a number-six pink fly. A fish took straight out about two feet beneath the surface ripping ten feet of line through my fingers on the take. It proved to be the strongest, wildest fish I've ever taken on the Umpqua and it nearly went over into the pool below before I could beach it. And, its adipose fin was missing, which I assumed made it a hatchery fish, since to mark fish they often remove this useless fatty fin.

Just as the fish was released, two steelhead rolled directly in front of me. The splashes were seconds apart and about six feet from one another. I waded straight out and using the same fly as before, made a long cast and to my decreasing amazement hooked another fish. It took about five minutes to release that one at forty yards.

I'd noticed earlier that another fisherman had been casting far down at the lower end of the hole. Now he was walking toward me. As he neared he spoke.

"Boy," he said, "you're doing OK."

"Yes," I answered.

"The fish seem to all be up here. Mind if I try it?"

"Not at all."

But unfortunately my friend's tackle was unequal to the job. He was only able to cast forty feet and the fish were at ninety.

Finally he said, "I notice I'm not getting out there as far as you. Maybe I should be using my weight forward line instead of this double taper."

"I would if I were you," I offered.

"But," he went on, "does your line float or sink?"

"Sinks."

"My weight forward line floats," he said. "So I don't know

whether to stick with my double taper, which sinks but doesn't cast far enough, or change to my other line which casts farther but doesn't sink."

"I don't know what to say," I sympathized. "You need both distance and depth here. Sounds like a Mexican standoff to me."

He stuck to his double taper and after I caught three more fish in rapid succession, he finally shrieked, "Now I know what these fish are doing. They're running up right under the willows on the other bank! I'll never get one!" Then, in a frenzy, he reeled in and left.

After that I hooked four more. In all it was what anyone would have to describe as an exciting afternoon—eleven fish landed out of fourteen hooked. Yellow flies, green, brown, orange, red, you name it they took it. And a day like that is not one in a million on the Umpqua either.

Other streams have summer runs, the nearby Rogue for instance. And along the Columbia drainage there are the Deschutes, Klickitat, Kalama, Wind and Clearwater rivers to name but a few. But the North Umpqua is the best and the reason, in a word, is management. The fishery is being protected and nurtured so that all may benefit.

Chapter Fourteen

NIGHT OF THE SALMON

It has been a clear, almost windless day in the Smith River Canyon. California's subtle fall has arrived, the most perfect time of year. A few miles from Jedediah Smith Park, below the Hiouchi Bridge, a sharp turn in the river tiered with bedrock shelves and undercut by caves is known to anglers as the Society Hole. It has not yet rained so the water is low and clear and in the main pool about a hundred and fifty king salmon can be seen circling restlessly. From the rocks on the north bank half a dozen anglers are fly-fishing. Among them is Bill Schaadt.

At 3:40 P.M. on this Monday of October 30, 1972, he cocks his massive wrist and drives a cast out over the pool, at the time merely another of the perhaps twenty thousand he will make this fall. His line swings in the gentle current, stops, and after a beartrap strike Bill has hooked another salmon.

Held aloft, the rod dips in long slow movements for nearly half a minute. Bill watches it critically to determine where the fish is hooked while keeping a tight line with his left hand. The late afternoon sun slants into the clear water and his eyes eagerly search the depths for a glimpse of the fish. Finally he anounces to Bob Tusken, who is fishing nearby: "It's fair and I think one of the big ones too!" Both fishermen see momentarily a great form twisting beneath them.

During the preceeding few days, when I'd been fishing Society too, we would notice among the salmon, all of which were large, two we thought were sixty pounds or more. They'd cruise by the ledge just outside the main school and if the sun was right and there was no wind, they could be clearly seen even in twenty feet of water. "There go the torpedoes," someone would say with quiet excitement whenever they passed. Speculation was constant over the possibility that one might be hooked.

Bill's fish, unperturbed, sounds beneath the ledges. It is a bad thing from the angler's point of view and everyone knows it because we'd all lost fish that had gone into the caves. But there is one chance because Bill has his boat tied close by. He rows into the pool so his line angles away from the sharp rocks but the salmon senses the place of safety and continues to burrow against the underwater cliffs. Bill remarks grimly, "I'll never land this one."

On the south bank of Society an immense gravel bar sweeps convexly from a riffle below the bridge in a full arc down to the Rip Rap Hole, a distance of some thousand yards. Bill beaches his boat at the one sandy spot on the stretch, which happens to be immediately opposite where he hooked his fish. From this purchase on dry land he exerts an exact pressure, impossible from the eight-foot boat that moves too easily under a strain.

Deliberately the salmon begins to move upstream, staying near the bottom, gaining line evenly. Bill knows he must follow and decides quickly to use the boat rather than run along the bank. From shore any snag would terminate the fight—he must get on top of the salmon. Two hundred yards of line have melted from the reel as Bill, fly rod between his legs, tip out over the stern, sends the little pram surging ahead with long powerful strokes.

The sun has dropped behind the high wall of redwoods but even in this shadowed light the tops of great boulders and a suggestion of terraqueous canyons can be seen. By this time Bill is up in what we call the corner, fully two hundred and fifty yards above the main pool. Like most others on the Smith, this hole is a nightmare of snags. The salmon finds a yard-wide crevice between two house-sized boulders, swims through it and out the other side. The line hangs up. Holding the rod lightly, Bill peers here and there into the depths. The daytime visibility of thirty feet or more is reduced in the gathering twilight so the deeper spots fade into blackness. The fish can't be seen and the line scrapes sickeningly against some ledge.

Bill maneuvers above the problem, working the boat back

and forth, finally regaining a clear line. Straining away from the rocks upstream he leads the salmon free only to have it circle around back through the crevice. Following his previous path, Bill clears the line again but the fish goes around and around the biggest rock, ever burrowing into this haven.

In time, the salmon leaves the boulders in a dash that takes him upstream toward the riffle. The actual rapid lies another two hundred yards off, but the fish strains into the heavy current, taking hundreds of feet of line. Bill cannot row strongly enough to maintain.

Turning abruptly, the salmon races back downstream, throwing a tremendous slack bow in the line. In seconds the fish is past the boat, then below it, veering into the narrow canyon, through it and out, speeding back toward the lower pool. Reeling with blinding speed, Bill sees his line pinpoint the crevice, drifts over, frees it straight to the fish and begins moving down until both angler and quarry are once again in the Society Hole. The salmon bores into familiar caves and once more the boat steers it into open water. It is a standoff.

All this while I've been fishing downstream in the Rip Rap Hole. Deciding I am skunked, I undertake the long walk back up to Society. Through the dusk Bill sees me on the gravel bar and calls out: "Get in your boat and come out here. You've got to try and see this fish before he gets off." Rowing out, I hang nearby, looking. Nothing.

"I can't do anything with him," Bill goes on. "Could be one of the torpedoes, I don't know. Took a small fly on an eight-pound leader. There's almost no chance of getting him. Wish we could get a look."

"Eight-pound?" I can't believe it.

"Had to. They just wouldn't take anything heavier in the clear water. This is the fifth fair one I've had this afternoon."

"It's too dark," I say. "We'll never see him unless he comes to the top. How long you had him?"

"About an hour and a half," comes the reply. "He's already been up into the riffle and back. He finds the snag up there. Got him out once but he can still do whatever he wants."

I sit for a moment and study the action. Bill holds the rod with strength, grace and knowledge. It bows deeply under all the strain an impossibly light leader can stand. I feel clearly the hopelessness of the situation. On high-quality fifteen-pound material, fully 75 per cent of the kings hooked on flies escape. Eight-pound? The odds are almost non-existent.

The salmon starts off again upstream and soon the leisurely move becomes a steaming run. Bill's boat surges away from me into the evening as the fish once again finds the crevice. Amazed at this display of sheer power I sit stunned, but knowing there isn't a thing to be done, I row ashore and wait on the beach. It is getting too dark to fish, so most of those who had been fishing earlier now stand by. Jack Geib has a Thermos of coffee so he, Bob Tusken and I talk it over.

We can barely make out Bill as he works once more to free the fish from the tangle of boulders. Succeeding, he comes toward us following the salmon which stops in the deepest water.

Suddenly there are voices behind us coming from a group of men who are trudging over the gravel bar to the river. They carry rods and tackle boxes.

"Look!" the first says. "A guy's got one on already."

"Already?" I look at Jack Geib. "Already? What is this, the night shift?"

"Glow-puppy boys," Jack laughs.

A glow puppy is a plastic lure that shines in the dark after being held under a light, much the same as do numerals on a clock. Legal fishing hours are from an hour before sunrise until an hour after sunset. When the water is low and clear, salmon generally spurn everything but tiny flies, so the lure fishermen use glow puppies, fishing them in the dark of early morning and late evening.

One of the glow-puppy boys slings his lure far out into the hole. "Say there," comes an anonymous warning, "this fella here's had a big salmon on for two hours now. If you cross him with that thing we'll cut your line." The caster backs away while others mingle around talking and drinking coffee.

Bill is perched on a mound of gravel somewhat above the water. I stand by, wondering at the precise pressure he keeps, the controlled give and take. Not a moment of relief is allowed the fish as it circles in deep water.

Someone gets a flashlight. Its beam spikes through the night, glancing from the water over to the redwoods beyond. Then another light is on, crossing the first. Bill's line shows clearly, making it possible to know just where the fish is. It starts to swing upstream.

"There he goes," Bill tells me. "The hell with him."

"Can't let him go after all this," I answer, running down to my boat. "Get in behind me. I'll row. It's the only chance."

The two of us sit as one in the eight-foot boat while I row stiffly toward the jumble of boulders.

"He knows these rocks," Bill says. "He goes into a deep crevice then out and around again."

The knot of onlookers moves jerkily up the gravel bar, stumbling on football-sized river stones. Now, four or five lights crisscross in the dark, illuminating Bill and me as if we were players on a stage. The clear water is penetrated easily by the moving beams of light, making me feel that we are floating upon eerie greenish transparent clouds. Below are large olive-colored rocks outlined by the flickering light. Still we can't see the fish but at least with the aid of lights Bill leads the salmon out of the boulders. It begins another fast run upstream.

"I just can't believe it," I say as the fish streaks up into the fastest part of the riffle. "Where is he getting that strength?"

I can't row fast enough to keep up while the salmon gains a hundred yards on us, nosing hard at the foot of the rapids. Keeping the boat in the slowest water near shore, he eventually comes abreast. The crowd is scant yards away so I call out: "Let us have a light, maybe we can get a look at this fish."

Taking the light I set it down as the fish turns and bolts back downstream. A chattering reel near my ear tells of the increasing distance between us and the fish. Things are out of control again as it enters the crevice.

With the current to help we aren't far behind, and as we come near I take up the light and play it down among the awful rocks. Every detail of the grotto reveals itself as the beam slices to the bottom.

"There he is!" I whisper, as a dark form glides under us and out of sight.

"Can you tell anything?" Bill asks.

"No. Could be forty or a hundred. It was just a glimpse."

Our speculation is cut short by the start of another terrific run downstream. I follow tiredly. It is a crisp, black night, clear and cold, stars flickering icily above. The lights bob and jerk far behind as the crowd stumbles over the uneven gravel bar. As we float over deep water, crowded blackly on all sides by towering redwoods, Bill's reel sounds its intake click.

When the lights catch up, the fish is holding at the upper end of the ledge. It circles toward the beach, than heads upstream.

"It can't be," I moan. "Not another run back up there."

Ignoring my plea, the salmon swims strongly away. With me rowing bow first, Bill holds his rod up over his shoulder, reeling blindly. Moans go up from the beach as once more the lights lag and swerve. I grab my flashlight to get some bearings just as the salmon finds the crevice again. He is through and out again before we even know it.

Bill clears his line as the salmon shoots back downstream past the group of assistants toward the main pool. What agony to be on shore, where every step in the dark becomes an effort over loose uneven rock. In the pool again the fish holds.

"Let's go in to the beach," Bill suggests. "I'll be all right if he stays here."

"OK," I agree. "I'll hang nearby in the boat just in case."

For an hour or more the fish alternately lunges, sulks and twists, staying in deep water. I beach the boat and stand by. A truck pulls off the North Bank Road and shines a spotlight down at us. We assume it is Grant King, with whom Tusken and I are staying.

"What time is it?" I ask Bob.

"Nine-thirty," comes the answer.

"Grant must be looking for us," I finish.

Jack Geib went home because he had to be at work early the following morning. Others drift off too, leaving myself, Bob and four or five men.

The fish runs tentatively upstream. There is no talking as I get in the boat and Bill stumbles in behind. Within a hundred yards the salmon stops and we come right over him. I pick up the light and look down. There he is, gray and indistinct, a large form undulating deliberately through the narrow beam of light. Bill sees him too.

"Damn!" he curses. "Just can't tell how big."

For a moment I think the line is going to his dorsal and I panic. It isn't unheard of for the hook to pull loose from one spot and lodge in another. But then the fish veers close and we both see that he is at least hooked up front.

"When he's tried everything else," Bill states, "he'll jump."

As Bill says this, the line starts slanting up.

"Here he comes!" Bill yells.

Inches from the transom an immense form lifts from the water in an arc which carries it clearly over the left oar even with our heads. I see the trajectory of its eye. Yells go up from the beach. The boat rocks crazily as spray drenches us. I think we are going over. It occurs to me also that the salmon could very well land in our boat.

There is pandemonium: Bill and I are wet and shaking, he is laughing, screaming and gesticulating all at once; I am stunned, the fish is streaking away at top speed and the lights on shore slash aimlessly at the dark. The salmon is a hundred yards below us before I have the presence of mind to go after it. Again it stops in the pool and Bill gets out on the sand.

"If I wasn't absolutely positive this fish took the fly," Bill says to me, "I'd break him right now. Hell, I'm tired and I'm not going back in the boat with him. If he goes in the snag again let him go."

"I'm sure he's a taker, Bill," I encourage. "I've been watching the rod and the fight and I don't think there's any doubt he's fair-hooked. Stay with him, this could be the big one."

Salmon are often foul-hooked by fishermen. Such fish are broken off immediately but occasionally the fish is hooked close to the mouth, which makes it hard to tell when playing it if it's really fair or not. I was more conscious of this than usual because I'd recently spent over an hour beaching a forty-pounder that turned out to have been hooked in the very end of its snout and had to be released.

Almost invariably though, a fair fish opens and shuts his mouth convulsively while shaking his head. A claim is sometimes heard that if the fly is close to the mouth, say in the chin or cheek, the salmon struck and missed but this is simply not the case.

"How many times have you gone to take a bite out of a sandwich and stuck it in your nose instead?" Bill will ask with a fierce glare.

All his monofilament backing is out now with the knot between it and more backing clearly visible off the rod tip. The diminishing gallery is leaving us with only two lights which Bob Tusken, and another man and I alternately hold trained on the rod so Bill can see how the fish is behaving. The knot approaches a little, then retreats.

"I can't understand why he won't break," Bill remarks to me. "I just know he's hooked in the mouth but he won't roll over. Watch now."

He increases pressure to the danger point so I can see the fish turn ever so slightly, but before the full turn, the salmon rights itself and regains several feet. This goes on for an hour.

All the while I watch Bill's moves, his hands, amazed. The left crooks itself around the rod below the first guide, lifting with unyielding pressure. He must risk the assumption the leader is in good shape and play the fish accordingly. He is on guard never to be caught unaware by a sudden rush.

Then the knot begins to pulse steadily away into the dark. The reel reverses spasmodically as line angles away in the nearly horizontal direction.

"He's heading for the chute," Bill says desperately. "He's

almost there and I can't turn him."

The chute is a narrow rock-strewn rapid which branches out of Society. It lies hard against the north bank holding about half the river's current. Studded with sharp irregular rocks, a fish may be counted as lost if he goes in.

"You can't get a fish through there in daylight," Bill moans in desperation. "He can't go down there, he just can't!"

"Should we go over in the boat?" I ask.

"No, I'll have to try to hold him. He's right on the lip. If I let up an ounce he'll just drift over."

The salmon holds on the brink of freedom for half an hour. The temperature is freezing and now that the battle becomes more psychological than physical, Bill is shivering. Someone brings a coat.

The flashlights are dimming. One is only a small simple handlight, the other a more powerful beam with a hinged spot and handle. We decided it best to use one at a time to conserve.

"He's breaking!" Bill says with guarded enthusiasm. Leaning on the rod first, then reeling down on slack, line comes back. The knot comes into the guides and disappears into the reel.

"This might be it," I say. "There's your shooting lead."

Indeed the salmon is close, perhaps fifty feet away, swimming downstream, parallel to the beach. We stumble and trip a hundred feet or more when the fish turns back toward the pool, only to again reverse himself and start down. The little gathering of anglers and spectators follows with difficulty like an odd disjointed toy being dragged around by a young child. The flashlights become weaker.

About then Sid Green shows up, an old friend of Bill's, who is staying with him at the time in the latter's trailer.

"What's goin' on?" he asks. "Got worried. Thought maybe someone was hurt when you all didn't come in tonight."

"Bill has had this fish since before dark," I reply.

"Well, why don't he pull the son-of-a-bitch in?" Sid half-smiles.

"Somebody take care of him," Bill mumbles over his shoulder, too concerned by now for joking.

"I'll go back and bring some coffee," Sid offers, moving off into the dark. "And let people know back at camp things are okay."

It is after midnight and the salmon is still strong. It begins thrusting its way further downstream in the near channel. Taking the reserve flashlight, I stumble along behind Bill trying to keep up. He moves with agility as always, keeping firm control of rod and line. The fish is picking up speed.

The Rip Rap Hole is three hundred yards away. Between lies a long flat, then a quick, short riffle.

"He wants to go over," says Bill finally.

We can hear powerful splashing off out in the dark. It is almost too shallow as the salmon wallows and thrashes violently. In strong starts he heaves downstream, throwing sheets of spray. I turn the light on the river.

"There it is!" yells Tusken. "Look at him go! He's over!"

With a good current behind him the fish is now in the upper end of Rip Rap, speeding for deep water. Tusken and I had surveyed the pool earlier from above with Polaroid glasses.

"What's there?" Bill demands quickly. "He's hung."

"Rocks and every damn thing," I answer nervously.

"Well, he's around a limb I think. Here, you take the rod and see what you can do."

I am wearing chest-high waders, while Bill has only low boots, so taking the rod I wade into the dark fearfully.

"I'm going for the boat," I hear Tusken say as he runs off into the night.

"Turn off the light and save it," I advise. "It won't do any good. I have to feel my way just the same."

The line is around something solid. I decide Bill is right in calling it a limb, because it feels somewhat spongy and the fish can take line at will. Wading out to within inches of my wader tops I hold the rod high. It is no use, I can't reach the snag and the salmon begins to run. Within moments the reel is chattering and I know the fish is more than a hundred and fifty yards off. I look at the reel. Not much line is left.

Behind me there are agitated voices and then a gravelly sound.

"Here's the boat!" Bill calls.

He climbs in and starts rowing out to me as I back up. Handing him the rod, I jump up, dragging myself over the transom, manage to get into the seat and grab the oars. Both lights glow dimly from the beach. We follow the line out past the obstruction as Bill clings to the yet reversing reel.

"Wait a minute, it's off! It's free!" Bill is excited. "Let's go!"

I row swiftly downstream close to the beach.

"Quick, give us one of the lights," I call.

At the center of the hole on its beach side, a boulder the size of an apartment house blocks the way of the shore-bound assistants. They have to work away from the river to get around it and then not much beach is left beyond. The fish pulls as strongly as ever, still heading down. Bill and I follow.

In the distance can be heard the roar of rapids.

"What's below us?" asks Bill.

"This is as far as I know it," I answer. "Except that I do know there's a nasty riffle we can't go over in the boat. The spot Grant King launches his boat on the other side is where we'll have to beach."

The roar of the rapids becomes ominously loud.

"He's heading for it," Bill laments. "What can I do?"

"I don't know," I reply. "Try giving slack, maybe he'll move back into the pool."

I turn my light on the line as it begins curving back upstream. Across the river Tusken and the others hold their light.

"Turn it off!" Bill yells. "Can't see!" Then, "It's working, he's going back into the pool. It's working!"

Line bellies around to come tight above us. It almost hisses.

"How can he do it?" Bill marvels, shaking his head. "Where is the energy coming from? Uh, oh, here he comes!"

The salmon is streaking wildly. It is hopeless to reel.

"He's going over!" Bill yells above the roar of water.

A shallow bay blocks our way.

"Here!" Bill commands. "Take the rod and run, I'll meet you below. It's too deep for me."

Floundering, I slash through the thigh-deep water barely able to stay upright. Line fairly screams off the reel. Reaching the beach at the head of the boiling rapid, I lurch absurdly into Bill as he takes the rod on the run. Suddenly, he is dashing back upstream past me. I think he's gone mad.

"The damn line's hung on a branch," he is screaming. "Oh! It's off!"

He then rushes past and I follow trying to direct the nearly dead light ahead. Two hundred yards later the salmon turns to face the current in the Simpson Park Hole.

We are alone in the quiet cold night when the light goes out. I am an exhausted, nervous wreck, but I know Bill is still intent on maintaining what I've come to think of as the Perfect Pressure. He repeats many times he just can't lose this fish after so many have done so much.

"It it gets off it won't be my fault," he says positively. The hook may pull out but I'm not going to break this leader."

Suddenly he is bathed in light as three cars come jouncing over the makeshift road along the gravel bar toward us. It is Bob Tusken, the fellows who'd provided the lights, and Sid Green.

Lights are everywhere. We can see the narrowness of the river. The speed of the current and the bottom all the way across. The salmon is clearly visible fifty feet out. I notice its great jaw gape open, then shut. The fish never loses cognizance of the current, never wavers, never falters, never turns. Now it simply pulls hard.

Bill is pulling too, and the fish comes a little, then veers sharply toward us. Bob waits tensely and I crouch at the water's edge. I'll be doing the tailing since I am in waders. But the salmon is swimming too fast as his belly touches gravel and he swerves downstream and runs strongly out a hundred feet or so. Nervous perspiration soaks my underclothes even in the chill of what now must be early morning.

"Coffee anyone?" Sid asks.

I have some and it helps as I sit for a moment in the protection of Sid's car. Typical of the river canyon, an icy breeze blows down the river. I take a cup of coffee and offer it to Bill.

"No, no, no, no, not now." Bill is agitated. He is feeling the pressure of so many depending on him. It is true, no one will leave until the end, whenever that might be.

Then a new light begins dancing on the trees beyond. Turning, I see up on the highway a car stopped, spotlight on.

"Sheriff or warden," I think. Then the car pulls into Simpson Park and down the road and comes to a stop behind us. Not knowing who it is, or caring by this time, I order: "Shine that spotlight out there on the fish!"

Evidently amazed that poachers could be so utterly blatant, the game warden complies. Someone goes over and explains. It is now quarter to three and it seems he isn't quite ready to believe the fish was hooked at twenty minutes to four on the previous day.

For over half an hour the salmon holds like a fixture in mid-stream. Sid falls asleep in the front seat of his car. Then, with agonizing slowness, it begins to come. But still it is upright, balanced. I ease into the water and kneel. A mere ten feet away the fish thrusts against tension. Inch by inch he is pulled closer. He never breaks, won't roll over, simply swims upright until his nose touches the beach. Like a mechanical monster facing a brick wall unable to think out a retreat, the salmon sits motionless as I grip it ahead of the tail. The warden lurches forward grappling, trying for a gill, and together we land the salmon.

It dies as Bill carries it into the glare of many headlights and lays it down. It is a darkish male of peculiar proportions, angular and bony. As there are athletes among men this surely is a superfish among salmon. In twenty-five years of angling I've never seen anything like this. I regard the fish with reverence, noticing in the strong light that its whole side ripples and convulses as if cramped. No doubt it is, for the fish has been fighting for eleven hours and thirty-three minutes.

"Look at this." Bill holds the fish's head up. His leader goes to a tiny fly in the left corner of its jaw. In the right corner is another fly to which he points, similar to the first.

"I caught and released this fish the other day," he says. "I remember it clearly because it was just a few days ago. I already had two big fish in the boat when I hooked this one. At the beach I just popped my leader and turned him around so I could keep fishing."

The next morning when the superfish pulls the scale down to forty-two pounds, six ounces, Bill can only shake his head.

"How I wish I had let it go," he says, "again."